THE AMERICAN VETERANS COOKBOOK

THE AMERICAN VETERANS COOKBOOK

A Collection of Recipes from Veterans and Their Families

*Terry P. Rizzuti and
R. E. Armstrong*

iUniverse, Inc.
New York Lincoln Shanghai

THE AMERICAN VETERANS COOKBOOK
A Collection of Recipes from Veterans and Their Families

Copyright © 2005 by Terry P. Rizzuti and R. E. Armstrong

iUniverse books may be ordered through booksellers or by contacting:

iUniverse
2021 Pine Lake Road, Suite 100
Lincoln, NE 68512
www.iuniverse.com
1-800-Authors (1-800-288-4677)

The American Veterans Cookbook: A Collection of Recipes from Veterans and Their Families contains 200 recipes contributed from veterans and their families living in many parts of the country, but also a few from around the world. We have used our best effort to insure accuracy and completeness in transcribing these recipes from digital and hardcopy formats, but we have not personally tried to cook and sample each recipe. Additionally, people's taste buds differ, as do ovens, crock-pots, measuring devices, etc. We therefore cannot guarantee accuracy or completeness, nor be held responsible for the cooking outcomes of preparing these recipes. However, it is our understanding and belief that these recipes have been "time-tested" in the kitchens of the homes of our contributors, and adjusted and perfected over the years. We also believe these recipes will appeal to most American families, and that many of them are appropriate for children.

ISBN: 0-595-34229-9

Printed in the United States of America

To America's Veterans and Their Families

Contents

PREFACE

Fifty percent of all author royalties from sales of *The American Veterans Cookbook: A Collection of Recipes from Veterans and Their Families* will be donated directly to the Armed Forces Veterans Homes Foundation, located in Suitland, MD. While the authors believe this organization is worthy of our support, we are not associated with it in any way whatsoever. This Foundation is a non-profit, non governmental organization that operates exclusively for charitable purposes and solely for the public welfare. The organization solicits, receives, manages and disburses financial resources by means of grants and awards to agencies nation wide that serve the needs of elderly and infirm veterans of America's armed forces.

The Foundation's primary objectives as stated on their website (vethomesfoundation.org) include the following: 1) to provide philanthropic support for and enhance the lives of elderly and infirm veterans requiring long term care, 2) to provide funding and services for both resident and operational needs at State Veterans Homes and National Retirement Homes, 3) to plan and execute a five-year, $30 million campaign for the Homes, and 4) to establish a permanent national endowment fund for the benefit of all Veterans Homes.

If sales of this recipe collection go well, we plan to produce new editions in the future to continue our fund raising efforts for programs and projects that benefit American Veterans and their families. We appreciate very much your contribution to this worthy goal on behalf of our nation's veterans who have sacrificed so much to ensure our American way of life. Some have sacrificed life or limb(s), others their professional careers and schooling; still others have sacrificed their physical and/or mental health. We as a nation have an obligation to this special segment of our population that absolutely must be expressed in heartfelt ways and actions. Please join us in doing just that.

INTRODUCTION AND ACKNOWLEDGEMENT

The authors very much enjoy cooking, as well as eating fine meals, but neither of us is a professional cook. We believe the art of cooking is all about creativity through experimentation and presentation. Like most fun things in life, we find that cooking can be messy and time consuming, but for those of us with a desire to enjoy life to the fullest, the end result is well worth the effort, more often than not.

Remember, we usually get out of something exactly what we are willing to put into it, so don't be afraid to try new things. Everyone's taste buds differ. Just because a recipe calls for a specific measurement or ingredient, that does not restrict you to using that exact amount or that particular ingredient. In fact, the authors rarely prepare the same recipe the same way twice in a row. So don't hesitate to change a recipe either. You may want to leave out certain ingredients or substitute others in their place. The name of the game is experimentation, and for what it's worth, this applies to life as well as cooking, so try to get all you can out of both.

We wish to thank everyone, veterans and family members alike, who shared recipes for this collection, including those whose names did not accompany their submissions. We have included individual names beside each recipe as our way of extending a special thanks to each and every one of you, our contributors. If we've overlooked anyone, please accept our heartfelt apology. We wish also to thank our friends and families for their support, some of whom contributed not only moral support and encouragement, but also recipes from among their own personal favorites.

TPR & REA   January 27, 2005

ABBREVIATIONS

doz.	Dozen(s)
lb.	Pound(s)
oz.	Ounce(s)
qt.	Quart(s)
tbsp.	Tablespoon(s)
tsp.	Teaspoon(s)

APPETIZERS

Salsa Ala Mel

This salsa is best served in the summertime using garden fresh ingredients.

2 large cloves of garlic, peeled and chopped small
1 medium white onion, peeled and chopped small
1 large (or 2 small) jalapeno peppers, chopped small with seeds
1 medium green pepper, seeded and chopped small
12 medium vine ripened plum tomatoes, diced with pulp and seeds
1 large (or 2 medium) zucchini squash (substitute cucumber if preferred), diced small with skin on (remove any large seeds)
1/2 cup of fresh cilantro leaves, chopped (do not use stems)
1/2 tsp. of salt
1/4 tsp. of black pepper
1/2 tsp. of ground cumin
1 and 1/2 tbsp. of olive oil
(For "over 21" recipe): 3 tbsp. Jose Cuervo Tequila

If you prefer a thinner, runnier salsa, you can add: 3 tbsp. of PACE brand picante sauce, medium flavor

Mix all the ingredients together in a bowl. Refrigerate at least 2 hours (or overnight) to let the Cuervo "do its stuff!" Serve with fresh tortilla chips.

Contributed by Melisa Cameron

Ground Turkey Taco Dip

1 lb. of lean ground turkey
2 cloves of garlic, chopped
1 medium white onion
1 medium green bell pepper
1 tsp. olive oil
1 can of pinto beans
1 bag of shredded low fat cheddar cheese
2 cups of fresh lettuce, chopped
4 or 5 small plum tomatoes, diced
2 to 3 tbsp. of fresh cilantro
Tortilla chips

Brown the ground turkey. Add the garlic (1 clove), onions, green pepper, and cook until tender. Set aside the cooked mixture.

In about one tsp. of olive oil, cook the remaining garlic and add the pinto beans. Stir until coated with oil, about 2 to 3 minutes. Using a masher, mash the beans into a paste stirring a couple more minutes.

In a 9x13 inch pan, spread the cooked beans evenly. Next, add the meat mixture evenly, and sprinkle on in order: cheese, lettuce, tomatoes, and cilantro. Serve with fresh tortilla chips as an appetizer.

This dip may be refrigerated overnight for use the next day (for parties), but best when served fresh. Serves 4 to 6 or more

Contributed by Melisa Cameron

Pork Spread

1/2 lb. of cooked pork roast
1/2 lb. of cooked ham
1 celery stalk
1 onion
Mayonnaise
1/4 cup of pickle relish

Grind or mince the pork, ham, celery, and onion. Then stir in enough mayonnaise to make a moist spreadable mixture. Blend in the pickle relish, and serve as a sandwich or as a cracker spread.

****

Pork Chili Sauce

2 lb. of ground pork (or sausage)
2 cloves of garlic, minced
1 onion, chopped
2 cans of diced tomatoes
6 to 8 oz. of chopped green chilies
2 tbsp. of chili powder
Salt and pepper to taste

Brown the meat in a skillet over medium heat then add the garlic and onions. Cook for about 15 to 20 minutes. Drain off the grease. Then mix the tomatoes, chilies, chili powder, salt, and pepper in a bowl. Pour this mixture over the meat. Bring it to a boil, reduce the heat, cover and simmer for an hour or more. Can be served as a dip with chips.

Contributed by Terry Rizzuti

Asian Pork Appetizers

2 lb. of lean pork, cut into small strips
1/4 cup of soy sauce
2 tbsp. of oil
2 cloves of garlic, minced
1/4 tsp. of dried hot pepper
1/2 tsp. of sugar
1/4 tsp. of anise seeds
1/8 tsp. of cloves
1/8 tsp. of cinnamon

Combine all of the ingredients, except the pork, in a bowl and mix well. Place the pork strips in the bowl and stir, making sure to coat each piece of meat. Cover the bowl and refrigerate for at least 2 hours. Thread the meat onto skewers and cook over a grill turning occasionally for 5 to 10 minutes or until the meat is cooked to your satisfaction.

Contributed by Terry Rizzuti

Avocado Salsa

Tomatoes
Purple onion
Green onion
Garlic cloves
Oregano
Cilantro
Jalapeno peppers
Avocado
Italian dressing

The amount of the ingredients used to make this salsa depends on the amount of salsa you want to make. Use more or less of each ingredient depending on your particular taste for that ingredient. Chop all the ingredients into small bits. Mix all the ingredients in a bowl, adding the avocado and Italian dressing last.

Contributed by Imelda Armstrong

Southern Style Veggie Dip

2 cans of black-eyed peas, drained
1 can of white hominy, drained
2 medium tomatoes, chopped small
1 bunch of green onions, chopped small
2 cloves of garlic, minced
1 bell pepper, chopped small
1 onion, chopped small
1/2 cup of parsley, chopped small (or dried)
1 small can of mild chilies
8 oz. of Italian dressing
Tortilla chips

Combine all of the ingredients in a large bowl except for the Italian dressing. Mix well then pour the salad dressing over the mixture. Cover and refrigerate to marinate for 2 to 4 hours. Drain and serve with tortilla chips.

Contributed by Imelda Armstrong

****

Green Chili Salsa

16 cups of tomatoes
12 garlic cloves
6 cups of green chilies
1 tbsp. of salt
1 large onion

Combine all the ingredients in a large bowl and mix well. Serve with your favorite chips.

Contributed by Patsy Lethgo

Mexican Fiesta Dip Mix

1/2 cup of dried parsley
1/3 cup of chili powder
1/3 cup of onion, minced
1/3 cup of ground cumin
1/4 cup of dried chives
1/4 cup of salt

Combine all the ingredients and mix well to make the spice for the dip, then store the spice in an airtight container. In a mixing bowl, combine the following ingredients:

3 tbsp. of Mexican Fiesta Dip Mix
1 cup of mayonnaise or low-fat mayonnaise
1 cup of sour cream or low-fat yogurt

Whisk the mixture until smooth. Refrigerate for 2 to 4 hours. Add the spice mix to make a quick and easy spicy dip. Serve with tortilla chips or fresh veggies.

Contributed by Patsy Lethgo

Mock Crab Dip

1 cup of Miracle Whip
1 and 1/2 cups of Monterey jack cheese, grated
1 and 1/2 tsp. of seafood seasoning
1 tsp. of Worcestershire sauce
1/4 tsp. of dry mustard
1 lb. of imitation crabmeat
Ritz crackers

Preheat the oven to 350 degrees. Combine the Miracle Whip, ¾ cup cheese, seafood seasoning, Worcestershire sauce, and mustard. Mix in the crab meat. Spoon the mixture into a casserole dish and sprinkle with remaining cheese. Bake 15 minutes. Serve with Ritz crackers.

Contributed by Patsy Lethgo

****

Mom's Cheese Dip

1 large can of Rotel tomatoes
2 tbsp. of chili powder
2 tbsp. of onion, minced
1 lb. of Velveeta cheese

Cook the first three ingredients in a saucepan over medium/low heat to reduce the liquid. Add the Velveeta cheese until melted. Can re-heat in a microwave.

Contributed by Patsy Lethgo

Pepperoni Dip

1 8-oz. package of soft cream cheese
1/2 cup of sour cream
1 tsp. of oregano
1/8 tsp. of garlic powder
1/8 tsp. of crushed red pepper
1/2 cup of pizza sauce
1/2 cup of pepperoni, chopped
1/4 cup of green onion
1/4 cup of bell peppers
1/2 cup of mozzarella cheese

Combine the cream cheese and sour cream. Add the seasonings and red pepper. Mix well. Spread evenly into a quiche dish. Spread the pizza sauce over top. Sprinkle with pepperoni, onion, peppers, and mozzarella cheese. Bake at 350 degrees for 10 minutes

Contributed by Patsy Lethgo

Angel Egg Puff

12 eggs
1/2 tsp. of salt
1 tsp. of baking powder
1/2 cup of flour
1 pint of cottage cheese
1/2 lb. of cheddar cheese, shredded
1/2 lb. of Monterey jack cheese
1/2 cup of melted butter
Paprika

Beat the eggs until they are light and fluffy. Add together and mix all the dry ingredients except paprika. Combine all in a large mixing bowl, including the cheeses and butter. Pour into a 9x13 inch baking dish. Lightly sprinkle with paprika for color. Preheat the oven to 350 degrees, and bake for 30 minutes

Contributed by Patsy Lethgo

****

Seafood Dip

24 oz. of cream cheese
6 oz. of crab meat, cooked
6 tbsp. of milk
2 tbsp. of Worcestershire sauce
Ritz or saltine crackers

Let the cream cheese soften to room temperature, then mix it with the crab meat, milk, and Worcestershire sauce. Put the mixture in a baking dish, and bake it in the oven preheated to 350 degrees for about 15 minutes. Serve with Ritz or saltine crackers or chips.

Scottish Highland Scones

1 cup of flour, un-sifted
3 tbsp. of sugar
2 tsp. of baking powder
1/2 tsp. of salt
1/3 cup of shortening
1/2 cup of currents
1/2 cup of quick cooking oatmeal
2 eggs, beaten

Stir the flour, sugar, baking soda, and salt together in a bowl. Stir in the shortening until the mixture is crumbly. Then stir in the currents and oatmeal. Add the eggs and stir until the mixture is moistened.

Lay the dough on a floured surface and knead lightly about 10 times. Roll or pat the dough into a 7-inch circle and cut it into 8 wedges. Place the wedges on a baking sheet about 2-inches apart. Bake them in an oven pre-heated to 450 degrees for about 8 minutes or until golden brown. Serve warm.

Contributed by Rick Dyer

SAUCES AND DRESSINGS

BBQ Sauce

1 cup of ketchup
Salt and pepper to taste
1 cup of red wine vinegar
1/2 cup of brown sugar
2 cloves of garlic, minced
1/4 cup of molasses
1/2 onion, diced
1 1/2 tsp. of liquid smoke

Combine all of the ingredients in a medium saucepan over high heat, and whisk until smooth. Bring sauce to a boil, then reduce heat and simmer uncovered for 30 to 40 minutes or until sauce has thickened. Use on pork spareribs or any of your beef, pork or chicken recipes. *Makes about 1 and 1/2 cups.*

Contributed by Patsy Lethgo

Korean Barbeque Sauce

1 cup of soy sauce
1/4 cup of water
1/2 cup of sesame seed oil
8 cloves of garlic, minced
1 tsp. of ginger
1 bunch of green onions, chopped
1 cup of sugar
Black pepper to taste

Mix all the ingredients together well. Marinade meat of choice for 24 hours before grilling.

Contributed by Terry Rizzuti

****

Green Chili Sauce

1 small onion, chopped
1 clove of garlic, minced
2 tbsp. of oil
1 tbsp. of flour
2 or 3 cups of broth of choice
1 cup of green chilies, diced
1 small tomato, peeled and diced
½ tsp. of cumin

Sauté the onion and garlic in the oil until soft. Stir in the flour and blend well. Simmer the mixture for a couple of minutes to "cook" the flour. Slowly add the broth, and stir the sauce until smooth.

Add the remaining ingredients, bring to a boil, reduce the heat, and simmer until the sauce has thickened, about 15 minutes. Serve in rice, over enchiladas, etc. *Yields 2 to 3 cups.*

Contributed by Patsy Lethgo

Vinaigrette Dressing

1 tbsp. of olive oil
2 tbsp. of lemon juice
1 tbsp. of Dijon mustard
3 tbsp. of chicken broth, fat free
Sea salt and fresh ground black pepper to taste

Mix all of the ingredients together well, then pour over salad.

Contributed by a member of the Vietnam Veterans of America

****

Home Made Chili Sauce

12 large tomatoes, chopped
3 onions, chopped
3 green peppers, chopped
1 bunch of celery, chopped
1 and 1/2 cups of sugar
1 cup of vinegar
2 tsp. of salt
1 tsp. of cinnamon
1/2 tsp. of black pepper

Mix all the ingredients in a saucepan over medium heat, and cook down until the mixture thickens and is a dark color. Pour into jars and seal. *Tastes great on red meat.*

Contributed by Patsy Lethgo

Thai Chili Sauce

1/2 cup of vinegar
1/4 cup of sugar
2 tbsp. of paprika
1/2 tsp. of flour mixed with 1 tbsp. of water
1 tbsp. of lemon juice
1/2 tsp. of chili peppers, minced
1/2 tsp. of salt
1/2 tsp. of red chili paste
2 tsp. of tomato paste
2 cloves of garlic, minced

Combine all of the ingredients in a small pot with 1/2 cup of water. Bring to a boil and stir well. Reduce the heat and simmer the mixture for about 5 minutes, stirring occasionally. Let the sauce cool, then refrigerate.

Contributed by Terry Rizzuti

****

Smoked Meat Rub

1/4 cup of brown sugar
1/4 cup of pepper
1/4 cup of paprika
1/4 cup of chili powder
1/8 tsp. of salt
1/2 tbsp. of mustard
1 tbsp. of garlic powder
3 tbsp. of onion powder

Rub the mixture on the meat and bake: (For chicken 400 degrees for 30 minutes.)

Contributed by Patsy Lethgo

Pork Roast Marinade

1/2 cup of ketchup
1/2 cup of water
1 clove of garlic, minced
1/2 tsp. of salt
2 tbsp. of brown sugar
1/4 tsp. of pepper
2 tbsp. of cider vinegar
1/8 tsp. of cayenne pepper
2 tbsp. of Worcestershire sauce

Marinate the pork overnight. Cook marinated pork in a crock-pot.

Contributed by Patsy Lethgo

ENTREES

Lone Star Chili

1 lb. of ground beef
1 onion, diced
1 tbsp. of fresh jalapeno pepper, diced
1 cup of water
1 tbsp. of white vinegar
1 tsp. of salt
1 15-oz. of can kidney beans with liquid
1 tsp. of chili powder
1 14.5-oz. can of peeled diced tomatoes
1/4 tsp. of garlic powder
1 8-oz. can of tomato sauce
1 bay leaf

Brown the ground beef in a large saucepan over medium heat. Drain the fat. Add the onion and pepper and sauté for about two minutes. Add the remaining ingredients and simmer for 1 hour, stirring occasionally. Serve with optional cheese, diced onion, and whole jalapeno garnish on top. Makes about 4 servings.

Contributed by Patsy Lethgo

Rib Eye Roast

5 lb. rib eye roast   1 large onion
2 oz. of butter   1 tbsp. of Worcestershire sauce
1 tbsp. of A-1 sauce   1 tbsp. of Teriyaki sauce
1/2 cup of chili sauce   4 tsp. of sea salt
1/2 tsp. of black pepper

Rub the roast with the salt, pepper, and butter, then brown quickly on all sides under the broiler. Mix the other ingredients together and pour over the roast. Preheat the oven to 325 degrees and bake the roast for about 20 minutes per pound for a rare roast. For best results always start with the meat at room temperature.

Chili Verde

5 lb. of lean roast beef (or a mixture of beef and pork), cut in bite size pieces and then browned
2 to 4 cloves of minced garlic, added to the meat toward the end of browning

Then add:

2 large cans of whole or diced tomatoes
1 large can of green chilies, rinsed
1 can of beef broth
1 large onion, sliced
1/2 cup of parsley, chopped
2 tsp. of cumin
1/4 tsp. of cloves
1 cup of dry red wine
Salt and pepper to taste

Cook on low heat for at least 2 hours or until the meat begins to fall apart. Can be served over rice, as a burrito stuffing when combined with rice and/or beans, as a taco stuffing, or inside an omelet.

Contributed by Diane Mercier

****

Chili Con Queso

1 lb. of Velveeta cheese, melted
15 oz. of chili with beans
4 oz. of green chili peppers, chopped
1 onion, diced

Mix all of the ingredients together and bake them in the oven preheated to 350 degrees for about 35 minutes. Serve with corn or tortilla chips.

Black Bean Chili

1 lb. of ground beef
1 cup of green onions, diced
1/2 cup of bell pepper, chopped
1/3 cup of carrots, shredded
1 15-oz. can of black beans, drained and rinsed
16 oz. of tomato sauce
1 15-oz. can of diced tomatoes
2 tsp. of chili powder
1 jalapeno pepper, seeded and diced
Sea salt and fresh ground black pepper to taste
Shredded or grated cheddar cheese

In a large pan or pot, brown the ground beef with the onions, bell peppers, and shredded carrots. When the meat is browned, drain off the fat and add the other ingredients, stirring well. Bring the chili mix to a boil, then turn the heat down and simmer covered for about 20 minutes. Serve with cheddar cheese or sour cream as a topping.

Contributed by Shawn Flanagan

Tex-Mex Pork and Zucchini

2 lb. of pork tenderloin, cubed
1 onion, diced
1 bell pepper, diced
2 zucchini squash, cut into bite size pieces
3 tomatoes, diced
1 tsp. of cumin
2 or 3 cloves of garlic, minced
1 can of whole kernel corn
Sea salt and fresh ground black pepper to taste

Brown the meat in a skillet on medium heat. Add the diced onion and bell pepper. Turn the heat to low, cover the skillet and continue to cook for about 15 minutes. Add the zucchini, tomatoes, cumin, and garlic, and cook covered for about 15 more minutes. Add the can of corn, salt, and pepper, and simmer covered for about 30 more minutes or until the zucchini is tender.

****

Arabian Meatloaf

1 cup of bulargeur wheat
1 and 1/2 lb. of lean ground beef
1 onion, chopped
2 bell peppers, chopped
Salt and pepper to taste
3 hard boiled eggs, chopped

Soak the wheat in 1 cup of water for about 30 minutes, then drain. Blend the wheat, ground beef, onion, peppers, and seasoning together. Put half of the mixture in a baking dish or pan. Place a layer of chopped hard-boiled eggs over the mixture. Put the remainder of the meat mixture over the hard boiled eggs and bake in the oven pre-heated to 350 degrees for about 45-minutes to an hour or until meatloaf is cooked.

Stuffed Bell Peppers

4 small bell peppers
15 oz. of chili with beans
1 can of Mexican style corn, drained
1 small Bag of corn or tortilla chips

Cut the tops off the bell peppers and clean out the insides. Cook the peppers in boiling water for about 15 minutes. In a pot or pan, combine the chili, corn and some crumbled chips and heat while stirring until it reaches a boil. Fill the bell peppers with the chili mix and serve with extra chips.

Contributed by Phil Huston

****

Spicy Southern Style Meatloaf

2 lb. of ground beef
1 lb. of ground pork sausage
1 onion, minced
1 bell pepper, minced
2 eggs, beaten
1/3 cup of ketchup
1/4 cup of brown sugar
4 cups of soft breadcrumbs
1/3 cup of maple syrup
3 tbsp. of Worcestershire sauce
2 tbsp. of hot sauce
1 15-oz can of tomato sauce

Stir all of the ingredients together except for the tomato sauce. Pat the mixture into a baking pan or dish, and pour the tomato sauce over the top. Bake in a preheated oven at 350 degrees for about 1 hour.

Contributed by a member of the Vietnam Veterans of America

Veal (or Chicken) Parmesan

Marinade 6 to 8 veal cutlets (or boneless/skinless chicken breasts) in Italian Dressing for 1 hour or more.

Coat both sides of the meat with Italian Bread Crumbs.

In a large skillet, sauté 3 minced garlic cloves in a mix of 3 tbsp. of olive oil and 3 tbsp. of butter.

Brown the meat on both sides, then place the browned meat in a large baking dish sprayed with non-stick cooking spray. Sprinkle the meat with red table wine. Then sprinkle the meat with dried oregano. Lightly coat the top of the meat with Marinara sauce. Sprinkle a mix of shredded Parmesan and Mozzarella cheeses over the meat.

Bake in the oven preheated to 350 degrees until done, about 15 minutes for veal, up to 30 minutes for chicken.

Contributed by R. E. Armstrong

****

Beef Pot Roast

1 3-lb. beef roast
3 or 4 potatoes, peeled and sliced thin
10 or more baby carrots, cut bite sized
1 onion, sliced
Salt and pepper to taste
3 cloves of garlic, minced
1/2 cup of beef broth

Spray a crock-pot with non-stick spray. Layer the vegetables in the bottom of the pot. Salt and pepper the meat to taste, then place on top of the vegetables and sprinkle with the minced garlic. Add the beef broth and cook on high heat for 1 to 2 hours, then reduce to low heat for 2 to 4 hours, or until done to satisfaction.

Contributed by Terry Rizzuti

Stuffed Rib Roast

5 lb. rolled rib roast
1/2 cup of onion, diced onions
2 cloves of garlic, minced
2 tbsp. of brown sugar
1 tbsp. of mustard
1/4 cup of water
1 tbsp. of Worcestershire sauce
1 cup of soft bread crumbs
Tony Chachere's Seasoning
3 oz. can of sliced mushrooms
1/2 cup of shredded cheese

In a bowl, combine the onions, garlic, brown sugar, mustard, water, Worcestershire sauce, bread crumbs, and seasoning. Spread the mixture over the unrolled roast. Drain the can of mushrooms and lay them on top of the mixture, then sprinkle with the cheese. Roll the roast and tie securely, place in a baking pan and bake in a preheated oven at 325 degrees for about 90 minutes.

Ray's Beef Stew

1 lb. of stew beef, cut into bite size pieces
1 cup of flour
3 cloves of garlic, minced
2 or more potatoes (depending on size)
10 baby carrots
1 large yellow onion, chopped
1/3 head cabbage, chopped
1 can of tomato soup
1 can of onion soup
1 can of beef broth
1 cup of red wine (or water)
Salt and pepper to taste.

Spray the bottom and sides of large crock-pot with non-stick cooking spray. Coat beef chunks with flour and layer on the bottom of crock-pot. Mince garlic and sprinkle over beef. Add a layer of potatoes and then a layer of carrots. Layer chopped onion over carrots then put in a layer of cabbage. Pour in the tomato soup, onion soup, beef broth, and red wine (or water). Add salt and pepper. Cover and cook on high for about 6 to 8 hours.

Contributed by R. E. Armstrong

Hot Dog Stew

8 beef hot dogs, cut into 1/2" pieces
2 tbsp. of flour
1/2 cup of water
3 potatoes, peeled and diced
Sea salt and black pepper to taste (optional)

Mix the flour and water until it is smooth. Brown the hot dog slices in an un-greased pan, then add the diced potatoes. Pour the flour and water mix over the hot dogs and potatoes, and add the sea salt and ground black pepper to taste. Cover the pan and simmer until the potatoes are cooked.

Contributed by Andy Hicks

Spicy Beef Ribs

5 lb. of beef short ribs (fat trimmed)
Hot pepper sauce to taste
1 tsp. of coriander
2 tsp. of cumin
3 cloves of garlic, minced
1 tbsp. of sea salt (to taste)
2 tbsp. of chili powder
1 tsp. of parsley
10+ oz. of chili sauce
1 onion, diced
1 cup of red wine
1/2 cup of water
1/2 cup of beef broth
1/2 cup of olive oil

Combine the hot pepper sauce, coriander, cumin, minced garlic, sea salt, chili powder, and parsley in a medium size bowl and mix well. Rub this mixture on both sides of the beef ribs, then place the ribs in a re-sealable plastic bag (or container with a cover). Refrigerate them for 1 hour or more.

Combine the remaining ingredients in the bowl to make a marinade. Save about 1 cup of the marinade for basting, and add the rest of the marinade to the ribs, letting them refrigerate for another hour. Remove the ribs and discard the used marinade.

Bake the ribs in the oven preheated to 375 degrees for 40 to 60 minutes, or until the ribs are cooked and still tender. Baste the ribs often with the additional cup of marinade and turn them at least once to brown them on both sides.

Contributed by a member of the Veterans of Foreign Wars

SOS

4 oz. of dried or smoked beef
2 tbsp. of butter
2 tbsp. of all-purpose flour
1 cup of milk
Salt and pepper to taste
1/2 tsp. of Worcester sauce (optional)
Toast or biscuits

Sauté the beef in butter until hot. Remove the beef and blend the flour into the butter. Pour in the milk and cook. Stir constantly until the mix is thick and bubbling, then slowly add the beef. Salt and pepper to taste, and add Worcester sauce for added flavor.

****

White Gravy SOS

1 lb. of ground beef or sausage
1 onion, diced
1 clove of garlic, minced
Cooking oil, butter or bacon grease
Flour
Whole milk
Salt and pepper to taste

Brown the meat in a skillet with the onion and garlic. Drain the meat mixture and set aside. Heat a small amount of oil (butter or bacon grease) in a skillet while stirring in enough flour to make a paste. Add the whole milk to the flour and stir while the gravy thickens. Blend the meat mix into the gravy and serve over toast or biscuits. Salt and pepper to taste.

Contributed by Terry Rizzuti

Asian Marinade Beef

1 to 2 lb. of beef, thinly sliced
2 to 4 green onions, chopped
3 or 4 cloves of garlic, minced
5 tbsp. of soy sauce
2 tbsp. of sesame oil
1/4 cup of sugar
1 to 2 tbsp. of toasted sesame seeds
1/8 tsp. of black pepper

Mix all of the ingredients together and marinade the beef in the refrigerator at least 8 hours in a covered container. Cook the beef by stir-frying in a hot, pre-heated skillet. Goes well with steamed rice.

Contributed by Terry Rizzuti

****

Easy Tex-Mex Stew

1 lb. of ground beef
1 onion, diced
1 clove of garlic, minced
1/2 cup of water
2 cans of diced tomatoes (about 30 oz)
1 16 oz bag of frozen stew vegetables
1 lb. of cooked new potatoes (halved)
8 to 10 oz of frozen corn
1 small can of chopped chilies, drained

In a large pot, sauté the beef, onion, and garlic stirring occasionally until the beef is browned. Then stir in the rest of the ingredients and bring to a boil. Reduce the heat and cover the pot. Simmer the stew for 5 to 10 minutes until all of the ingredients are heated.

Contributed by a member of Vietnam Veterans of America

Beef Egg Rolls

1 lb. of ground beef
1 can of sauerkraut, drained
1 lb. of bean sprouts
2 or 3 green onions, minced
2 tsp. of cornstarch
1 tsp. of sugar
1 tsp. of ginger
2 to 3 tbsp. of soy sauce
1 tbsp. of sesame seeds
1 lb. of egg roll wrappers

Brown the beef and then drain off the grease. Mix in all of the other ingredients except the wrappers and sauté to blend the flavors while stirring well. Cut the wrappers according to the size you want to make the egg rolls. Spoon the ingredient mixture into the center of the wrappers. Roll the mixture in the wrappers. Moisten the edge of the wrappers with water and seal. Deep-fry the egg rolls for about 3 to 5 minutes or until brown. Serve with spicy Asian mustard.

Bubba's Quiche

12 bacon slices, cooked crispy and crumbled
1 cup of shredded Swiss cheese
1/3 cup of onion, chopped
2 cups of milk
1/2 cup of Bisquick
4 eggs
1/4 tsp. of sea salt
1/8 tsp. of black pepper

Grease a 10" pie pan and sprinkle in the crumbled bacon, cheese and onion. Put the milk, Bisquick, eggs, salt, and pepper into a blender and blend for 1 minute on high speed. Pour into the pan and bake in an oven preheated to 350 degrees for about 50 minutes or until cooked throughout. Let it stand and cool for about 5 minutes before slicing. For extra flavor, top with medium to spicy salsa.

Contributed by R. E. Armstrong

Peppered Steaks

2 to 3 lb. of top quality steaks
1/2 cup of butter
1/4 cup of fresh parsley, minced
1/4 cup of minced onion
1/2 tsp. of dried mustard
1 tsp. of black pepper, freshly ground
2 tbsp. of Worchester Sauce

With a sharp knife make small slits in both sides of the steaks to better allow the marinade to soak into the meat. In a pot, combine the butter, parsley, onion, mustard, pepper, and Worchester sauce. Stir while heating until butter melts and the ingredients are blended together.

Pour about 1/3 of the mixture into a container to be used after the steaks have been cooked. Brush the butter mixture on both sides of the steaks and place them on a clean, preheated grill. Brush the butter mix on the steaks frequently while they are cooking.

When the steaks are done to your satisfaction, place them on a serving platter and drizzle the reserved butter mixture over them.

Contributed by Terry Rizzuti

Boudreaux's Blackened Cajun Steak

4 to 6 good quality filet mignons
2 to 4 tbsp. of melted butter
1 or 2 bottles of Chef Paul's (or other favorite) steak blackening spice

Heat a cast iron skillet over an outside burner until it's hot. Then brush melted butter on one side of the fillets and sprinkle liberally with steak blackening spice. Place the steaks spice side down in the hot skillet. Then brush butter on the topside of the steaks and sprinkle that side liberally with blackening spice.

After searing the spices on the bottom side of the filets, turn the steaks over in the pan to sear the other side. As soon as both sides of the filets have the spices seared on, remove them from the pan and finish cooking them on a grill until they are done to your satisfaction. *Note: It is best to sear the filets out of doors because they will create a lot of smoke.*

Contributed by R. E. Armstrong

Pickle's Crowd Pleasin' Chili

4 lb. of ground beef

2 large white onions, diced

Chili powder

Ground red pepper

1 bottle of beer, Budweiser (optional)

1 medium jar of hot cherry peppers with juice

3 lb. of ground sausage (hot or sweet)

4 bell peppers, diced

Cayenne pepper

2 20-oz cans of red beans

4 large cans of tomato puree

Mix the ground beef and sausage together in a large pot and sprinkle liberally with chili powder, cayenne pepper, and ground red pepper. Add the onions and bell peppers and brown the meats.

Add the cans of red beans, tomato puree, and the jar of hot cherry peppers with the juices and stir well. Let simmer for 30 minutes then add one bottle of Budweiser beer (optional). Stir well. Salt and pepper to taste, then cover and simmer for another 30 minutes, stirring occasionally.

Serve with saltine crackers or crusty Italian bread. This chili is "very hot" and should be served with plenty of bread and cold beer or other cold drinks. Depending on the bowl size this should make about 25 to 30 servings.

Contributed by Lawrence Pichulo

Southwest Casserole

1 lb. of ground beef	1 yellow onion, chopped
1 tomato, chopped	1 bell pepper, seeded and chopped
2 cloves of garlic, minced	1 cup of shredded cheddar cheese
1 can of chili beans	1 package of cornbread mix

Brown the ground beef in a skillet then drain off the grease. Add the chopped onion and garlic. Sauté for about 5 minutes then stir in the bell pepper and tomato. Add the can of chili beans with the juice and mix all the ingredients together well.

Pour the mixture into a casserole dish or baking pan that has been sprayed with non-stick cooking spray. Sprinkle cheddar cheese on top of the mixture.

Prepare the corn bread mix according to the directions on the package. Pour the corn bread mix over the top of the casserole mixture. Place in a preheated oven and follow the corn bread baking directions on the package (or bake at 350 degrees for about 20 minutes).

Contributed by Imelda Armstrong

Cheese-Stuffed Chicken Rolls

2 tbsp. of dried tomatoes (not oil pack)
4 skinless, boneless chicken breast halves
2 tbsp. of all-purpose flour
1/4 tsp. of salt
1/8 tsp. of pepper
1/3 cup of fine bread crumbs
2 tbsp. of Parmesan Cheese
1/2 tsp. of paprika
1 egg
4 oz. of sharp Cheddar cheese
1 tsp. of dried fine sage, crushed
1 tbsp. of margarine or butter, melted

Option: you can use anything to stuff the chicken—try ham and cheese, spinach, asparagus, etc.

Soak the tomatoes in enough water to cover for 10 minutes. In a small bowl, place the dried tomatoes (pat dry with paper towels). Finely chop the tomatoes and set aside.

Place each chicken breast half between 2 pieces of plastic wrap. Pound to 1/8 inch thickness.

In a small shallow bowl, combine the flour, salt, and pepper. In another small shallow bowl, combine the breadcrumbs, Parmesan cheese, and paprika. In another small bowl, slightly beat the egg.

Cut the cheddar cheese into four 3x1x1/2-inch pieces. Place a cheese stick on each pounded chicken breast half. Sprinkle each with some chopped dried tomatoes and sage. Fold in the sides of each chicken breast and roll up tightly. Roll in the flour mixture, egg, and then breadcrumb mixture.

Arrange the chicken rolls, seam side down, in a 2-quart rectangular baking dish. Drizzle the chicken rolls with melted butter. Bake, uncovered, in a 350 degree oven 20 to 25 min. or until the chicken is tender.

Grilled Orange Chicken

4 to 6 boneless, skinless chicken breasts
1/3 cup of concentrated orange juice
1/4 tsp. of red pepper flakes
1/2 tsp. of sea salt
3 tbsp. of teriyaki glaze
2 tbsp. of brown sugar
1 tbsp. of grated ginger

In a large re-sealable plastic bag combine all the ingredients (except the chicken) and mix well. Add the chicken, seal the bag and shake to coat the chicken breasts. Refrigerate and let marinade for about 1 hour. Spray the cold grill with non-stick cooking spray and heat to medium temperature. Remove the chicken from the bag and discard the marinade. Cook about 15 to 30 minutes, turning occasionally until the chicken is done to your satisfaction.

Contributed by Terry Rizzuti

****

Lime/Ginger Chicken

4 chicken breasts
3 zucchini, sliced
4 portabella mushrooms, sliced
1/2 tsp. of grated ginger
1/2 cup of cilantro, chopped
1/2 cup of lime juice
1 and 1/2 tsp. of lime peel, grated
Salt to taste

Mix all the ingredients except the chicken, zucchini and mushrooms. Marinate the chicken breasts in the mixture. Drizzle with oil, and grill. Toss the zucchini and portabella mushrooms with your favorite seasoning, and grill. Slice the grilled chicken and serve with the vegetables over rice.

Easy Chicken Chili

1 red bell pepper, diced and seeded
1 yellow bell pepper, diced and seeded
1 yellow onion, diced
1 tbsp. of olive oil
1 tsp. of chili powder
1 tsp. of cumin
2 cups of chicken, cooked and chopped
About 30 oz. of chicken broth
About 30 oz. of pureed tomatoes
About 30 oz. of diced tomatoes with mild green chili peppers
1 can of black beans, rinsed and drained

Cook the peppers and onions in olive oil over medium heat for about 5 minutes or until tender. Add the chili powder and cumin and cook for about 1 minute more. Add the chicken broth and tomatoes and bring to a boil. Reduce the heat and simmer for about 20 minutes, stirring occasionally. Add the black beans and cook for about 10 minutes longer. Serve with your favorite crackers or bread.

****

Fried Turkey Breast(s)

Turkey breast(s)
Sea salt and ground black pepper to taste
Flour
Milk
Olive oil

Slice the turkey breast(s) across the grain into thin strips. Sprinkle the turkey to taste with sea salt and fresh ground black pepper, then dip in flour coating both sides. Dip the turkey in milk then again in the flour, again coating both sides. Heat the olive oil in a large skillet and fry the turkey breast(s) on both sides until browned. Drain and serve while still warm.

Chicken Tetrazzini

4 boneless, skinless chicken breasts cut into 2" strips
1 cup of chicken broth
1/2 cup of dry white wine
1 onion, finely chopped
1/2 tsp. of salt
1/4 tsp. of dried thyme
1/4 tsp. of pepper
2 tbsp. of fresh parsley, minced
8 sliced mushrooms
3 tbsp. of cornstarch
1/2 cup of water
1/2 cup of half and half
8 oz of 2"-spaghetti pieces, cooked
1/2 cup of Parmesan cheese

In a slow cooker, combine the first 8 ingredients. Cook on low heat 4 to 5 hours. Turn to high heat. Add the mushrooms. In a small bowl, dissolve the cornstarch in water; stir into slow cooker. Cover and cook on high heat 20 minutes. Stir in the half and half, cooked spaghetti, and half the cheese. Cover and heat on high 5 to 10 minutes. Spoon into serving dish; sprinkle with remaining cheese.

Contributed by Patsy Lethgo

Chicken with Lime Sauce

4 skinless, boneless chicken breasts
1 lime, juiced
3/4 cup of apple juice
2 tsp. of cornstarch
1 chicken bouillon cube

Spray a large skillet with Pam. Heat over medium heat before adding the chicken breasts. Cook for 8 to 10 minutes or until tender; brown evenly. Remove and keep warm.

Combine the lime juice, apple juice, cornstarch, and bouillon cube in a bowl. Add to the skillet and cook, stirring until thick. Spoon the sauce over chicken to serve.

Contributed by Patsy Lethgo

Teriyaki Chicken

Put 4 skinless/boneless chicken breasts in a freezer bag or bowl with cover. Combine the following ingredients in a mixing bowl to make the teriyaki marinade.

1/2 cup of brown sugar
2 tsp. of white vinegar
2 tbsp. of olive oil
1/2 cup of soy sauce
3 cloves of garlic, minced
1/2 tsp. of ground ginger
2 tsp. of sugar

Pour the marinade over the chicken breasts, making sure to coat each one. Seal the container and refrigerate for 4 to 6 hours. Then, either fry the chicken breasts in a large pan using a mixture of equal parts butter and olive oil, or cook the chicken breasts on a grill until done. Serve with rice or other favorite side dishes.

Contributed by Terry Rizzuti

Chicken Marsala

4 skinless, boneless chicken breasts
3 or 4 cloves of garlic, minced
2 tbsp. of butter
2 tbsp. of olive oil
Flour or Italian breadcrumbs
1/2 cup of chicken broth
1/2 cup of Marsala wine
1 cup of sliced mushrooms
Sea Salt to taste

In a large pan, sauté the minced garlic in butter and olive oil. Coat the chicken breasts with flour or Italian breadcrumbs. Brown the chicken breasts on both sides. Add the chicken broth, Marsala wine and mushrooms to the pan. Simmer about 5 minutes on both sides or until the chicken is done. Salt to taste and serve with favorite side dishes.

Contributed by R. E. Armstrong

Chicken Enchilada Casserole

Taco chips
3 lb. of chicken, cooked and shredded
2 cups cheddar cheese, shredded
1 can of tomatoes
1 onion, chopped
2 cloves of garlic, minced
1 can of green chilies
Chile powder to taste
1 can of cream of mushroom soup
1 can black olives, diced

Layer the chips, chicken, half the cheese, tomatoes, onions, garlic, chilies, and chili powder in a 9x13 pan. Spread the soup over the top. Sprinkle with cheese, chili powder, and diced black olives. Bake at 400 degrees for 1 hour. May cover with foil (tent-style).

Contributed by Patsy Lethgo

Chicken Fricassee

Basic Ingredients:

4 boneless, skinless chicken Breasts
1 can of reduced fat cream of chicken soup
1/2 soup can of water
1/2 cup of onions, chopped
1 tsp. of rosemary
1 tsp. of thyme
1 tsp. of salt
1 tsp. of paprika
1/4 tsp. of freshly ground black pepper
1 tsp. of lemon juice

Chive Dumplings Mix:

3/4 tsp. of salt
2 tsp. of baking powder
1 and 1/2 cups of flour
3 tbsp. of shortening
2 tbsp. of dried chives
3/4 cups of skim milk

Spray a crock-pot with non-stick cooking spray. Place the chicken in the crock-pot. Mix the remaining basic ingredients together and pour over the chicken. Cover and cook on low heat for 6 to 8 hours.

About 1 hour before serving, prepare the chive dumplings as follows: Mix the first three ingredients and shortening. Add the chives and milk and combine well. Drop by the teaspoonful onto the hot chicken and gravy. Cover and cook on high heat for 45 to 60 minutes.

Serve with mashed potatoes and vegetables, or over hot, cooked noodles.

Contributed by Patsy Lethgo

Chicken Tortilla Pasta

2 or 3 boneless, skinless chicken breasts
Salt and pepper to taste
Chili powder
2 tbsp. olive oil
1/2 small white onion, chopped
2 cups of sliced mushrooms
1/4 cup of Velveeta light cheese
5 or 6 small plum tomatoes, diced
Cooked Pasta (mostaccioli or penne)
Tortilla chips, broken
Fresh cilantro

Broil or grill the chicken breasts until cooked. Season them with salt, pepper, and chili powder as desired.

In olive oil, cook the onions and mushrooms to desired tenderness. Add the Velveeta cheese, stirring constantly until melted. Add the diced tomatoes, and cook only until the tomatoes are warmed.

Slice the cooked chicken breasts and arrange on a plate over cooked pasta. Pour the cheese sauce over the chicken and cooked pasta. Top with broken tortilla chips. Garnish with fresh cilantro if desired. Serves 2 or 3 people.

Contributed by Melisa Cameron

Chicken Jambalaya

1lb. of boneless, skinless chicken breasts

3 cups of cooked rice

1 red bell pepper, seeded and chopped

1 14-oz. can of tomatoes

1/2 cup of tomato paste

1 tbsp. of dried parsley

1/2 tsp. of dried oregano

1 tsp. of cayenne pepper

1 lb. of shelled and de-veined shrimp

1 green bell pepper, seeded and chopped

1 onion, chopped

1 can of beef broth

4 cloves of garlic, minced

1 and 1/2 tsp. of dried basil

1 tsp. of hot sauce

1/2 tsp. of sea salt

Cut the chicken into bite size pieces and put into a crock-pot. Add all the other ingredients except the shrimp and rice. Keep the shrimp refrigerated until time to use. Cover the crock-pot and cook on low heat for 8 hours or on high heat for 4 hours. Add the shrimp to the crock-pot during the last 30 minutes of cooking. Stir in the cooked rice before serving.

Contributed by R. E. Armstrong

Chinese Chicken Salad and Dressing

Chicken breast, cooked and sliced into bite sizes
Lettuce
Red cabbage
Julienne Carrots
Fried noodles
Sesame Seeds
Mandarin orange wedges
Chives

The following dressing pulls it all together:

1/2 cup of mayonnaise	5 tbsp. of rice vinegar
2 tbsp. of sugar	2 tbsp. of sesame oil
1 tbsp. of soy sauce	1/4 tsp. of garlic powder

Combine all the dressing ingredients in a medium bowl and mix with an electric mixer until the mixture is well blended and the sugar is dissolved. Chill. Pour over the salad ingredients and toss.

Contributed by Patsy Lethgo

Kernal's Chicken

6 to 8 boneless, skinless chicken breasts
2 packages of dry Italian dressing
3 tbsp. of flour
2 tsp. of salt
1/4 cup of lemon or vinegar
2 cups of beer
Aunt Jemima Pancake Mix
2 tbsp. of oil

Mix the dressing, flour, salt, and lemon or vinegar into a paste and apply over the chicken. Cover and refrigerate 2 hours or over night. Prior to cooking, dip the chicken in the beer and dust with Aunt Jemima Pancake Mix, and allow to set for at least 5 minutes. Brown the chicken for 5 minutes per side in hot oil. Then bake at 350 degrees for 30 minutes.

Contributed by Patsy Lethgo

Quick and Easy Jambalaya

1 lb. of spicy sausage
1 cup of bell pepper, diced
1 cup of onion, diced
1 tsp. of olive oil
30 oz. of un-drained stewed tomatoes
1 and 1/2 cups of water
2 cups of white meat turkey or chicken, cooked and diced
1 tbsp. of Cajun seasoning
3 cups of uncooked white minute rice
Hot-sauce to taste

In a large pan or pot, sauté the sausage, bell pepper, and onion in heated olive oil until the sausage is cooked. Then add the un-drained tomatoes, water, turkey (or chicken) meat, and Cajun seasoning. Mix well and bring to a boil. Stirring in the rice, reduce the heat and cover. Let it simmer for about 5 minutes and remove it from the heat. Add the hot sauce. Let the Jambalaya stand covered for about 5 minutes then serve with hush puppies, corn bread or other favorite bread.

Contributed by R. E. Armstrong

Chicken Enchiladas

2 doz. Tortillas, dipped in hot oil
3 bunches of green onions, chopped
Chicken meat, cooked and shredded
Cheddar cheese, grated

Fill the tortillas with the above ingredients. Roll the tortillas up and place them seams down in a 9x13 pan. Warm the tortillas in the oven.

Mix together:

1 can of cream of mushroom soup
1 can of cream of chicken soup
1 pint of sour cream
1 can of chopped green chilies

Pour the mixture over the tortillas. Top with grated cheese. Bake at 350 degrees for 30 minutes.

Contributed by Patsy Lethgo

Mexican Chicken

1 fryer chicken, boiled
1 medium onion, chopped
1 lb. of Velveeta cheese
1 can of cream of chicken soup
1 can of cream of mushroom soup
1 can of Rotel
Dorito chips, crushed

Pull the chicken off the bone after boiling. Put the chicken in a 9x13 pan with the onion. Cover with cheese. Mix together the soups and Rotel, and pour over the chicken. Cover with crushed Doritos, and bake at 375 degrees for 20 to 25 minutes.

Contributed by Cheryl Moody

Sweet and Sour Chicken, Crock Pot Style

3 medium potatoes, peeled and thinly sliced
4 boneless, skinless chicken breasts
1 cup of orange juice
1/2 cup brown sugar, packed
1 tsp. of leaf basil
1/4 tsp. of nutmeg
2 tbsp. of cider vinegar
Dried parsley flakes
1 17-oz. can of sliced peaches, drained

Place the potatoes in a crock-pot. Arrange the chicken breasts on the potatoes. Combine the orange juice, brown sugar, basil, nutmeg, and vinegar. Pour over the chicken. Sprinkle with dried parsley flakes, cover and cook on low heat for 6 to 8 hours.

Remove the chicken and potatoes from the sauce and arrange on a warm platter. Turn the crock-pot to high heat, add the peach slices to the sauce, and heat until serving temperature. Pour the sauce over the chicken and potatoes, and garnish with chopped parsley. Makes about 8 servings.

Contributed by Patsy Lethgo

Wally's In-Between-Wives Skillet Casserole

1 lb. of turkey, ground
2 tbsp. oil
1 can of Campbell's beef with barley soup
1 can of unsalted cut green beans
2 cups of water
1/2 cup of elbow macaroni

Brown the turkey in heated oil in a large skillet or saucepan. Drain the meat and save half the turkey for Wally's next day salad recipe. Combine the remaining turkey with the soup, green beans, and water. Bring the mixture to a boil, stir then add the macaroni. Simmer the mixture for about 8 to 10 minutes. Serves one heavy eating bachelor or can be divided into two portions in case you have a date who is a light eater.

Contributed by Walter Waldau

****

Battered and Fried Rattlesnake

Rattlesnake meat, cleaned and cut into medallions about 1/2" thick
Sea salt and ground black pepper to taste
Cornmeal
Buttermilk
1 garlic clove, chopped
Olive oil

Season both sides of the meat with sea salt and fresh ground black pepper, then coat with cornmeal. Dip the meat in buttermilk, and again coat it with cornmeal. In a large skillet, sauté the garlic in olive oil for about 2 minutes, then cook the rattlesnake meat on both sides until it begins to turn a golden brown.

Contributed by an Oklahoma Veteran

Pork Tenderloin Roast

1 to 2 lb. pork tenderloin roast
1 tbsp. of vegetable oil
1 onion, sliced
2 and 1/2 cups of warm water
1 1-oz. package of Au Jus gravy mix
2 cups of cold water

Heat the oil in a Dutch oven and brown the tenderloin on all sides. Add the onion and sauté for 3 minutes being careful not to burn them. Add 1/2 cup of warm water and let it completely cook down (evaporate). Repeat this three more times.

Stir the gravy mix and 2 cups of cold water in a bowl. Pour it over the meat and bring it to a boil. Cover the Dutch oven and place in a preheated oven at 350 degrees for one hour. Add 1/2 cup of warm water and let it roast another hour.

Serve with noodles or mashed potatoes. Can also add potatoes or squash to cook along with the meat.

Contributed by Patsy Lethgo

Spicy Sausage Roux

2 lb. of lean pork sausage   1/4 cup of olive oil
1/4 cup of butter   1 tbsp. of Worchester sauce
Jalapeno pepper sauce to taste Flour (as much as needed)
Salt and pepper to taste (optional)

Brown the crumbled sausage in a skillet, then pour the meat and grease into a colander. Run hot water over the meat to get rid of all the grease and let it drain.

While the meat is draining, make the roux by adding oil, butter, Worchester sauce, and jalapeno pepper sauce to the skillet. Combine all the ingredients and heat over medium heat. Add salt and pepper if you like.

When these ingredients are hot, whisk in flour slowly until the mixture is about the consistency of thin paste. Continue to whisk the mixture while slowly pouring in about 1 and 1/2 cups of milk. You may need more or less milk depending on the consistency. The mixture will get thicker as it cooks. When the roux mixture is the consistency of gravy, stir the meat back into it. Once the sausage is reheated spoon the roux mixture over fresh biscuits, canned biscuits or English muffins.

Contributed by Bill Garbett

Easy and Delicious Chicken

4 to 6 chicken breasts
8 oz. of Italian-style dressing (may use fat free)
1 can of cream of chicken soup
1 cup of chicken broth
8 oz. of cream cheese
1/2 tsp. of dried basil
1/2 tsp. of dried thyme
Salt and pepper to taste

In a slow cooker, combine the chicken breasts and the Italian style dressing. Cook on low heat for 6 to 8 hours. When the chicken is tender, drain most of the dressing and discard. Shred the chicken meat and return to the slow cooker.

Combine the soup, broth, cream cheese, basil, thyme, salt, and pepper. Pour the mixture over the chicken in the slow cooker and cook for 1 more hour on low heat. Serve over pasta or rice if desired. Enjoy! Makes 4 to 6 servings.

Contributed by Patsy Lethgo

Baked Ham

1 uncooked ham with bone in it, any kind or size that fits in your pot
1 or 2 liters of Sprite, 7-Up or Ginger Ale
1/2 cup wine (optional)
Water
1/2 cup of orange or pineapple juice
1/2 cup of brown sugar
1 can of sliced Pineapple, 4 slices
Whole cloves
Maraschino cherries, optional

Coat a large pot with olive oil, and place the ham inside with fat side up. Pour in the Sprite or 7-Up for a sweeter taste, or Ginger Ale for a more tart taste. Pour in the wine, then fill the pot with enough water to cover the ham by about 1 inch. Bring the ham to a boil on top of the stove and then cover and reduce the heat to the lowest simmer you can achieve. Occasionally wiggle the ham around to keep it from burning on the bottom. When the meat just starts to pull away from the bone, remove the ham, place it fat side up in a baking dish and let it cool a little.

Meanwhile, mix the orange or pineapple juice, the brown sugar, and the juice from the canned pineapple. Score the top of the ham in a diamond pattern and insert the cloves in the corners. Arrange the pineapple slices on top of the ham, stabilized with toothpicks, and place the cherries in their centers. Baste the ham liberally with some of the brown sugar mixture.

Bake in the oven preheated to 350 degrees for approximately 30 to 45 minutes, basting every 15 to 20 minutes until the pineapple just begins to brown. Remove and serve.

Contributed by Terry Rizzuti

Baked Ham and Cheddar Cheese

8 to 10 oz. of ham, cooked and diced
8 to 10 oz. of small broccoli florets
4 cups of frozen hash brown potatoes with onions and peppers (thawed)
8 oz. of shredded cheddar cheese
4 eggs, beaten
2/3 cup of milk
Salt and pepper to taste

Coat an 8" square baking dish with non-stick cooking spray or butter. In a large bowl, mix the ham, broccoli, and potatoes, stirring well. Put half of the potato mixture in the baking dish, and top it with half of the cheddar cheese. Put the rest of the potato mixture on top of the cheese layer. Then sprinkle on the rest of the cheddar cheese.

Beat the eggs in a bowl, adding the milk, salt, and pepper. Blend well and pour it evenly over the potato mixture. Bake in the oven preheated to 375 degrees for about 40 minutes. Let it cool for 5 to 10 minutes before serving.

Contributed by Terry Rizzuti

Jalapeno Ham Steak

2 tbsp. of jalapeno pepper jelly
2 tbsp. of chopped cilantro (optional)
1 lb. slice of fully cooked ham steak

While the grill is heating up to medium heat, put the jalapeno jelly in a microwave safe bowl and microwave it for about 25 to 30 seconds, depending on how much power your microwave has. Add the cilantro (optional), stirring to mix it well.

Make sure the ham is dry, then place it on the grill over medium heat. Brush the topside of the ham with about half of the jalapeno jelly and let it cook for about 6 to 8 minutes until it is heated. Then turn the ham steak over and brush it with the remaining jalapeno jelly. Grill the ham for another 6 to 8 minutes or until it is done to your satisfaction.

Contributed by Terry Rizzuti

Crock-Pot Pork Roast

1 5-lb. pork loin roast
1 clove of garlic, slivered
1/2 tsp. of sea salt
1/4 tsp. of black pepper
2 onions, sliced
2 cloves of garlic, chopped
2 bay leaves
1 tbsp. of soy sauce
1/2 cup of water

Make small slits in the pork roast and insert the slivers of garlic. Rub the roast with salt and pepper. Broil the roast in the oven for about 20 minutes to remove the extra fat.

Spray the crock-pot with non-stick spray, then layer the bottom with one of the sliced onions. Add the pork roast and top with the remaining onion slices, then add the other ingredients. Cover and cook on low heat for about 8 to 10 hours or on high heat for 5 to 6 hours. *Use your cooking judgment, as crock pots vary.*

Skillet Ham and Beans

1 lb. of cooked ham, cut bite size
1 tbsp. of olive oil
1 onion, chopped
2 cloves of garlic, minced
1 can of kidney beans, rinsed and drained
1 can of white beans, rinsed and drained
1 bell pepper, chopped
1/2 cup of brown sugar
1/2 cup of ketchup
2 tbsp. of cider vinegar
2 tsp. of dry mustard

Heat the olive oil in a large pot or skillet until it is hot. Sauté the onion and garlic for about 3 minutes, stirring to keep them from burning. Add the kidney beans, white beans, bell pepper, brown sugar, ketchup, vinegar, and mustard, and mix them well. Add the cooked and trimmed ham to the bean mixture, and simmer for about 5 minutes or until the sauce begins to get thicker and all of the ingredients are heated. Stir occasionally to keep the ingredients from sticking and burning.

Contributed by Andy Hicks

Asian Barbeque Pork

3 lb. pork tenderloin
1/4 cup of sherry
1/2 tsp. of sea salt
1/2 tsp. of black pepper, freshly ground
2 cloves of garlic, minced
1/2 tsp. of grated ginger
1/2 cup of soy sauce
1/4 cup of sugar

In a bowl, mix all the ingredients except the pork loin. Blend well, then add the pork loin making sure to turn the meat so it is all coated in the marinade. Cover and refrigerate for at least 2 hours. Put the pork loin in a baking dish and bake in the oven preheated to 375 degrees for 1 hour. Baste the pork with the marinade several times during baking. Check for doneness before serving.

Contributed by Terry Rizzuti

****

Baked Ham with Marmalade/Mustard Glaze

5 lb. boneless ham, fully cooked
18 oz. jar of orange marmalade
1/2 cup of stone ground mustard
2 cloves of garlic, minced
2 tbsp. of dry mustard
1/2 tsp. of ground ginger

Preheat the oven to 350 degrees. Place the ham fat side up on a rack in a baking pan. Score the ham with a sharp knife. Mix the remaining ingredients until they are well blended, and set aside half of the mixture for a reserve to be served with the finished ham. Brush the ham with the remaining mixture. Bake the ham for about 2 hours, brushing with the marmalade mixture about every 15 minutes. Remove from the oven and let stand for about 10 minutes. Serve the ham with the reserved marmalade mixture as a topping.

Chinese BBQ Ribs

This amount of spareribs will yield about 24 ribs.

5 lb of spareribs
1tbsp. of honey
2 cloves of garlic, minced
1tbsp. of grated fresh ginger, or 1 tsp. of dried ginger
2 tbsp. of ketchup
2 tbsp. of red wine
2 tbsp. of soy sauce
2 tbsp. of hoi sin sauce

Preheat the oven to 300 degrees. Cut the spareribs into individual ribs. Place on a rack in a baking pan and bake for 45 minutes. Combine the remaining ingredients in a small bowl. Brush the sauce lightly onto the spareribs and roast the ribs another 30 minutes. Turn the ribs and brush them with the sauce again. Bake another 30 minutes until well browned.

Contributed by Patsy Lethgo

****

Pineapple Pork Chops

4 pork chops
1/4 cup of flour
2 tbsp. of olive oil
4 canned pineapple rings
1/3 cup of pineapple juice

Coat the pork chops in flour, and brown them in olive oil in a pan. Once they are browned on both sides, top each chop with a pineapple ring and pour the pineapple juice into the pan. Cover the pan and simmer slowly until the chops are cooked.

Pork Chops (or Chicken) and Wild Rice

4 thin pork chops or small chicken breasts
1 package of Uncle Ben's Long Grain & Wild Rice, Original Recipe
1 can of Campbell's Golden Mushroom Soup
1 small jar or can of sliced mushrooms (discard liquid)

Cook rice according to directions on the box. Meanwhile, mix the soup, mushrooms and half a soup can of water in a bowl and set aside. Lightly coat or spray a medium size baking dish or pan with olive oil. Pour the cooked rice in the baking dish, spreading it evenly, and lay the pork chops side-by-side on top of the rice. Pour the soup mixture over the top of the pork chops and rice, spreading it evenly. Place in the oven preheated to 350 degrees until the pork chops or chicken breasts are thoroughly cooked, approximately 45 minutes to 1 hour. *A good indication that the dish is done is when the edges of the soup liquid begin to brown and get crispy.*

The rice portion of this recipe can be doubled easily for larger crowds, and the pork chops or chicken breasts increased to 6 if you use a larger baking dish. Also, the recipe can be varied by browning the pork chops or chicken breasts beforehand, and/or by adding sliced onion and your favorite herbs or spices, such as black pepper and garlic, either during the browning or during the baking phase.

Contributed by Terry Rizzuti

Dr. Rudy's Spare Ribs

5 to 6 lb. of pork spare ribs
2 onions, sliced
2 bay leaves
2 tbsp. of vinegar
12 oz. of peach preserves

2 cloves of garlic, crushed
2 tbsp. of olive oil
2 tbsp. of soy sauce
14 oz. of ketchup

Trim the fat off the ribs and boil them in a pot of water, adding the sliced onions, 1 clove of crushed garlic, and the bay leaves. Boil the ribs for 30 to 45 minutes until tender. Drain the water from the ribs.

Brown 1 of the garlic cloves in olive oil in a saucepan or pot on low heat. Add the soy sauce, vinegar, ketchup and peach preserves. Stir and let boil for about 10 minutes.

Place the ribs in a baking pan and brush with half of the sauce. Bake uncovered in the oven preheated to 350 degrees for 30 minutes. Baste the ribs with the remaining sauce and turn them so both sides get browned. Bake for another 30 minutes.

Contributed by Dr. Rudy Abiera

Mexican Skillet

1 lb. of pork, cubed
1 medium onion, diced
2 medium potatoes, pealed and cubed small
1 12-oz. can of Rotel chopped tomatoes and chilies
1 6-oz. can of diced chilies
1 can of water
1 tsp. garlic salt
1 12-oz. bag of shredded cheese

Brown the meat and the onion. Add the potatoes, the can of Rotel tomatoes and chilies, and a can of water. Simmer on a low heat until the potatoes are completely cooked, then add the rest of the ingredients and stir well. After everything is cooked, sprinkle the cheese over the top and cover until the cheese melts. *Serves 2 to 4 people.*

Contributed by George Horgan

****

German Stew

8 to 10 small red potatoes
1 large jar of sauerkraut, rinsed
1 cup of apple juice
1 apple, wedged
1 onion, wedged
1 and 1/2 lbs. of Bratwurst, or smoked sausage
1 tsp. of caraway seeds

Place all the ingredients except the potatoes in a casserole. Bake covered at 350 degrees for 30 minutes. Add the potatoes and cook another 30 min, or until the potatoes are tender. *Serves about 6 people.*

Contributed by Patsy Lethgo

Green Chili Stew

2 lb. of cubed pork (beef or chicken) 2 large tomatoes, peeled and chopped
2 potatoes, peeled and chopped 1 large onion, chopped
3 cups of broth of choice 2 cups of green chilies, chopped
1 cup of water 2 tbsp. of vegetable oil
1/2 tsp. of ground cumin 1 tsp. of garlic, chopped
Sea salt to taste

Brown the meat in oil. Add the onions and garlic, and sauté until the onion is soft. Remove the meat and onion from the pan.

Add the cup of water to deglaze the pan. Combine the pan drippings and the rest of the ingredients in a Slow Cooker and simmer on low heat for approximately 6 to 8 hours (or on high heat for approximately 4 hours). Serve with warm tortillas.

Contributed by Patsy Lethgo

Philippine Noodles (Pansit)

4 small packages of mung bean noodles
1 onion, sliced
2 cloves of garlic, minced
2 tbsp. of olive oil
2 cups of chicken meat, cut bite size
1 cup of celery, chopped
1 cup of mushrooms, chopped
1 can of chicken broth
2 tsp. of paprika
Salt, pepper and soy sauce to taste
Dash of accent (optional)

In a large bowl, soak the dry noodles in warm water for 5 minutes, then cut with scissors and drain them in a colander. In a large pot, sauté the onions and garlic in oil for 2 minutes over medium heat. Add the chicken and cook until the meat is no longer pink. Stir in the celery, mushrooms, and chicken broth.

Raise the heat and bring to a boil. Reduce the heat and stir in the drained noodles, paprika, salt, pepper, soy sauce, and accent. Cover and let stand for 5 minutes to let the noodles soak up all the liquid. Add more chicken broth if the noodles seem too dry. Stir and serve.

Contributed by Imelda Armstrong

Scottish Eggs

1 and 1/4 lb. country style or herbed sausage
1 tsp. of crumbled dry sage
1/2 tsp. of crumbled dry thyme
1/4 tsp. of cayenne pepper
4 large eggs, hard-boiled
1/2 cup of all-purpose flour
2 large eggs, beaten lightly
1 cup of breadcrumbs
Enough cooking oil to deep fry the eggs

In a large bowl, combine the sausage, sage, thyme, and cayenne pepper. Blend well then divide the mixture into 4 equal portions. Flatten each portion into a thin round shape, and enclose one of the boiled eggs in one of the sausage rounds, patting the sausage into place.

Roll the sausage-coated eggs in the flour, shaking off the excess. Then dip them in the beaten raw eggs, letting the excess drip off. Roll the coated eggs gently in the breadcrumbs to coat them well.

Heat about 2 and 1/2 to 3 inches of oil in a deep fryer or pan to about 350 degrees. Fry the sausage until cooked, about 10 minutes. Dip the eggs from the oil with a slotted spoon and place on paper towels to drain off excess oil.

Contributed by Junny Jackson

Broiled Crab

1 lb. of fresh or frozen (thawed) crab meat
1/2 cup of butter
1 tbsp. of vinegar
1 tsp. of tarragon

Rinse and drain the crab meat, then put it in a shallow casserole dish. Mix the melted butter, vinegar, and tarragon, and pour it over the crab meat. Broil the crab meat for 12 to 15 minutes or until it is lightly browned.

****

Baked Halibut

1" thick Halibut steak(s)
Salt and pepper to taste
1/2 cup of breadcrumbs
2 cloves of garlic, minced
1/4 cup of olive oil
1/4 cup of Parmesan cheese
1/8 tsp. of dried thyme
Lemon wedges (optional)

Place the steak in an oiled shallow baking pan. Sprinkle with salt and pepper. Combine the breadcrumbs, garlic, oil, cheese and thyme to a thick paste and pat onto the surface of the steak. *Makes enough paste for 6 steaks.*

Bake in a preheated 450 degree oven for 14 minutes per inch of thickness of fish, or until the fish is no longer translucent and flakes when tested with a fork. Garnish with lemon wedges

Contributed by Patsy Lethgo

Grilled Citrus Salmon

2 salmon filets
1/8 tsp. of sea salt
1 tsp. of chives
1 tsp. of lemon juice
1/4 tsp. of lemon peel, grated
2 tbsp. of butter, softened
1 tsp. of dill

Spray the cold grilling surface with nonstick cooking spray. While the grill is heating, combine all of the ingredients except the salmon in a bowl and mix well. When the grill is heated spread about half of the mixture over one side of the salmon filets. Place the filets on tin foil, then on the grill with the mixture side up and cook for about 5 minutes. Then turn the filets over on the tin foil and spread the remainder of the mixture on top of the filets. Cook for about 5 more minutes or until done to your satisfaction.

Contributed by Terry Rizzuti

Shrimp and Noodles

1 lb. of fresh or frozen (thawed) shrimp, peeled and de-veined
1 tbsp. of lemon juice
1/2 tsp. of chili powder
1/4 tsp. of cumin
Sea Salt and black pepper to taste
3 cups of water
6 oz. of oriental flavored ramen noodles
1 or 2 green onions, diced
16 oz. of salsa (mild to hot)
1/4 cup of fresh cilantro
1 15-oz. can of black beans, rinsed and drained
1 8-oz. can of whole kernel corn, drained
Shredded or grated cheddar cheese

Combine the shrimp, lemon juice, chili powder, cumin, salt, and pepper. Stir well to coat and let set for 15 to 20 minutes, stirring occasionally. In a large pan or pot, bring the water to a boil and stir in 1 of the flavor packets that come with the ramen noodles.

Break up both packages of noodles and stir them into the boiling water. Cook the noodles for about 1 minute at a boil then add the shrimp and boil for about 2 more minutes until the shrimp turn pink. Stir in the green onions, salsa, cilantro, black beans, and corn. Simmer until all the ingredients are heated, and serve with a sprinkle of cheddar cheese for a topping.

Contributed by Shawn Flanagan

Alaskan Shrimp Salad

Steam: 2 pounds of cocktail shrimp

Gather: Pepper, beau monde, lettuce, and crackers

Meanwhile, combine the following in a large bowl:

2 cups of mayonnaise
1 pint of alfalfa sprouts, chopped
1/2 cup of pickle relish
1 package of frozen early peas (thawed, rinsed and drained)
1/2 Bell Pepper, diced fine
2 cups of celery, diced fine
Juice of 1/2 lemon

Mix all the ingredients and season to taste with pepper and beau monde. Serve on a bed of lettuce with crackers. Arrange the shrimp around the outside.

Contributed by Patsy Lethgo

****

Italian Shrimp

1 lb. of shrimp, shelled and de-veined
1 clove of garlic, minced
1 tbsp. of olive oil
28 oz. of canned Italian style tomatoes
1 tsp. of Italian seasoning

In a pan or pot, stir-fry the garlic in heated olive oil for a couple of minutes until it is cooked. Add the tomatoes and Italian seasoning and simmer until the sauce begins to thicken, breaking up the tomatoes. Then add the shrimp, and simmer for about 5 minutes longer or until the shrimp are cooked. Serve over rice or pasta.

Grilled Lemon Fish

6 oz. of tilapia or other light tasting fish
1 tbsp. of olive oil
1 tbsp. of lemon juice
1 tsp. of lemon peel, grated
1 tsp. of marjoram, diced
1 tsp. of parsley, chopped
2 tbsp. of minced pecans (optional)
1 shallot (or small onion), minced
1/4 tsp. of sea salt
1/4 tsp. of black pepper, fresh ground

Mix all the ingredients (except for the fish and oil) in a bowl to make a marinade, cover and let refrigerate for 2-4 hours. When you are ready to cook, spray the grilling surface with a non-stick cooking spray or wipe with olive oil, then heat up the grill to a medium heat. Brush oil on both sides of the fish filets and then place them in a shallow glass dish. Spoon the marinade on top of the filets, spreading evenly. Place the filets on the grill, topping side up, and close the grill, or cover the filets with a foil tent. Grill the filets for about 15 to 20 minutes or until fish is cooked in the thickest parts.

****

Lemon Shrimp and Pasta

10 oz. of ravioli, freshly cooked and drained
10 oz. of small shrimp, shelled, de-veined and cooked
10 oz. of Alfredo sauce
1 tbsp. of lemon juice
1 tsp. of lemon peel, grated
1/2 cup of parsley, freshly chopped

In a saucepan, combine the shrimp, sauce, lemon juice, and lemon peel to make a sauce. Heat over low heat, stirring frequently until heated. Do not let the sauce boil. Spoon the sauce over the pasta, and sprinkle with the chopped parsley.

Crab Cake Mix and Sauce

Mix:

1 Egg
1 lb. of crabmeat
Dash of Tabasco
1 oz. of heavy cream
Pinch of black pepper
1 tsp. of Coleman's dry mustard
1 oz. of chopped parsley
1/4 tsp. of salt
Pinch of cayenne pepper
1/4 cup of flour

Combine all the ingredients, shape into balls, and refrigerate. Fry in a non-stick pan with a little bit of oil on low temperature until golden brown on both sides.

Sauce:

2 shallots, chopped
1 cup of red wine
1/2 cup of heavy cream
1 lb. of butter
1/2 lemon, juiced

Heat the shallots and red wine together on medium heat until the liquid is half gone. Add the heavy cream; and simmer for 10 minutes on medium heat. Dice the soft butter, and whisk it in a little bit at a time. Add the lemon.

Contributed by Patsy Lethgo

Deep Fried Catfish

4 whole catfish, about 1 and 1/2 lb. each (or 8 filets)
2 eggs
Dash of Worcestershire sauce
Dash of hot sauce
2 and 1/2 cups of milk
1 cup of yellow cornmeal
1/3 cup of all-purpose flour
Salt and pepper to taste
1 tsp. of lemon pepper
2 qt. of peanut oil
8 scallions
3/4 cup of Miracle Whip
1/2 cup of mayonnaise
1/4 cup of pickle relish
1/4 cup of onion, finely chopped
3 tbsp. of fresh lemon juice

Tartar Sauce:

In a medium bowl, fold together the Miracle Whip, mayonnaise, relish, onion, and lemon juice. Cover and refrigerate until ready to use.

Catfish (skinned and beheaded):

In a bowl large enough for the fish, combine the eggs, Worcestershire, hot sauce, and milk. Beat until frothy. In a shallow dish large enough for the fish, whisk together the cornmeal, flour, salt, pepper, and lemon pepper.

With a small knife, score both sides of the catfish four times across, deeply, about 1 1/2 inches apart. Dip the catfish in the egg mixture then dredge it completely with the cornmeal mixture, evenly coating the fish. Set aside.

(continued on next page)

In a large pot or deep fryer, heat the oil to 325 degrees. Add the fish, one at a time for whole fish (two at a time for filets), and cook for 7 to 8 minutes, or until golden brown and crisp. Remove the fish and place on paper towels to drain. Serve with scallions and tartar sauce. *Serves four.*

Contributed by Terry Rizzuti

****

Cajun Fried Catfish

1 lb. of catfish (or tilapia)
3 tbsp. of flour
3 tbsp. of corn meal
Sea salt, black pepper and cayenne pepper to taste
3 tbsp. of olive oil

Combine the flour, corn meal, salt, black pepper, and cayenne pepper in a dish large enough to allow the fish filets to be rolled in the mixture. Coat the filets with the mix and shake off the extra. In a large skillet, heat the olive oil then add the fish, cooking it over a medium heat. Fry the fish for about 3 minutes on each side or until it is browned on the outside and cooked to your satisfaction.

Contributed by R. E. Armstrong

Easy Chicken and Seafood Gumbo

1 cup of bell pepper, diced
1 cup of onion, diced
2 cloves of garlic, minced
2 tbsp. of olive oil
1 tbsp. of flour
3 cups of chicken broth
15 oz. of diced canned tomatoes
1 package of frozen gumbo vegetables
1/4 cup of quick cooking rice
2 tsp. of Cajun seasoning
12 oz. of canned white meat chicken
6 oz. of canned crabmeat (or small shrimp)

In a large pot or pan, sauté the bell pepper, onion, and garlic in the olive oil until they are tender. Then stir in the flour, then the chicken broth, undrained tomatoes, gumbo vegetables, Cajun seasoning, and rice. Bring to a boil then reduce the heat, simmering covered for about 10 minutes, or until the gumbo vegetables are cooked. Then stir in the chicken and crabmeat (or small shrimp) and simmer for about 5 minutes more until all of the ingredients are heated.

Contributed by Shawn Flanagan

Easy Seafood Chowder

12 oz. of fish filets, cut into bite size pieces
12 oz. of frozen hash browns with onion
1 cup of water
1 10-oz. can of cream of potato soup
12 oz. of evaporated milk
2 tsp. of fresh dill, chopped
2 or 3 bacon slices, cooked crispy and crumbled
Sea salt and fresh ground black pepper to taste
2 oz. of pimentos, diced

In a large pot or pan, combine the hash browns and water and bring to a boil. Reduce the heat and cover, letting it simmer for 5 to 10 minutes or until the hash browns are tender. Then stir in the can of soup, evaporated milk, dill, bacon, sea-salt, and fresh ground black pepper. Bring the mixture to a boil, then add the fish and diced pimentos and reduce the heat. Cover and simmer for about 5 minutes or until the fish is cooked and flakes easily.

Contributed by a member of the Disabled American Veterans

Salmon Quiche

10" unbaked pie shell
1 10-oz. package of frozen chopped spinach
1 and 1/2 cups of shredded cheese
3 oz. of softened cream cheese
Salt to taste
1/2 tsp. of thyme
1 15-oz. can of pink salmon, drained
1 cup of milk
4 eggs, beaten

Bake the pie shell in an oven preheated to 375 degrees for about 10 minutes. Cook the spinach according to the instructions on the package and drain. Combine the spinach, shredded cheese, cream cheese, salt, and thyme. Drain the salmon and mash it, then layer it into the pie shell. Layer the spinach mixture over the salmon. Beat the milk and eggs together and pour over the spinach and salmon. Bake in the preheated oven for about 40 to 50 minutes until done. Let stand 10 to 15 minutes before serving.

Mexican Style Catfish

6 catfish or tilapia filets
1 cup of corn chips, finely crushed
2 tsp. of chili powder
Sea salt and black pepper to taste
3 tbsp. of lime juice
1 tbsp. of olive oil
1 cup of salsa

Combine the corn chips, chili powder, salt, and pepper in a shallow bowl. Mix the lime juice and olive oil in a separate shallow bowl.

Cut the fish filets in half, length-wise and dip them in the lime juice and olive oil mix. Then roll the filets in the corn chip mix to coat them well. Place the filets in a lightly greased baking dish or pan (or cook on the grill), and sprinkle any remaining corn chip mix over them.

In the oven preheated to 450 degrees, bake the filets for about 10 to 15 minutes or until the filets are crisp and golden. Serve the filets with warmed salsa for a topping.

Contributed by Shawn Flanagan

Grilled BBQ Shrimp

1 lb. of big shrimp, peeled and de-veined
1/2 cup of favorite BBQ sauce
Metal or wood skewers
Non-stick cooking spray for grill

In a plastic bag or sealable container, marinade the shrimp in half of the BBQ sauce for about 1 hour. Put the shrimp on skewers (soak wood skewers in water for 20 to 30 minutes before using), and place them on a grill cooking rack that has been sprayed with non-stick cooking spray. Discard the BBQ sauce the shrimp had marinated in, and using the remaining half of the BBQ sauce, brush the shrimp heavily on the top side then turn over and brush sauce on that side. Grill the shrimp for 4 to 6 minutes or until they are cooked.

Contributed by Mike Sovick

****

Drunken Shrimp

2 lb. of shrimp, shelled and de-veined
2 cans of your favorite beer
3 tbsp. of pickling spice
1 lemon, sliced
1/2 tsp. of sea salt

Pour the beer into a pot or pan and add the pickling spice, lemon slices, and salt. Heat until the pot is steaming, then add the shrimp making sure there is enough liquid to cover all of them. Cook until the shrimp turns pink then remove them from the pot and drain.

Contributed by Shawn Flanagan

Texas BBQ Shrimp

20 shrimp, shelled and de-veined
2 tbsp. of ketchup
1/3 cup of red wine vinegar
1 cup of olive oil
16 oz. of tomato sauce
3 cloves of garlic, minced
1/4 cup of minced cilantro
2 tsp. of sea salt
1 tsp. of black pepper

Combine the ketchup, vinegar, oil, and tomato sauce in a bowl with a cover and mix well. Mix in the garlic, cilantro, sea salt, and black pepper and stir well. Add the shrimp, making sure they are covered by the BBQ sauce and chill covered for 2 to 4 hours, stirring frequently to make sure all the shrimp marinade. Place the shrimp in a baking dish and cook under the broiler for 3 to 5 minutes per side or until the shrimp turn light brown.

Contributed by a Texas Veteran

Ginger Crab

1-2 lb. of crab meat, cooked
2 tsp. of cooking sherry
1 egg, beaten
2 tsp. of cornstarch mixed with water to make a paste
4 tbsp. of olive oil
1 tbsp. of grated ginger
4 green onions, chopped
1 tbsp. of soy sauce
1 tsp. of brown sugar
5 tbsp. of stock

Blend the sherry, egg, and cornstarch paste in a bowl, and marinade the crab meat for about 15 minutes. Then heat the olive oil in a pan, and stir fry the crab meat with the ground ginger and green onions for about 3 minutes. Add the soy sauce, sugar, and stock, and blend well. Bring the mixture to a boil, then simmer covered for about 3 to 5 minutes.

Contributed by Mike Sovick

****

Sautéed Quail

Quail meat
3 tbsp. of butter
2 cloves of garlic, minced
1 onion, chopped
Teriyaki Sauce
Salt and pepper to taste

Heat the butter and sauté the garlic for about 2 minutes. Add the quail meat, cover and cook at medium heat for about 6 minutes. Stir, add the onion, cover and cook for about 4 more minutes. Remove the cover, add the teriyaki sauce, stir and sauté for about 2 more minutes. Salt and peeper to taste.

Fried Quail, Dove or Squirrel

Seasoned salt
1 egg, beaten
1/2 cup of milk
Pancake flour

Blend the egg with the milk. Sprinkle the meat liberally with the seasoned salt. Then soak the meat overnight in the egg and milk mixture. Drain, dip the meat in the flour and fry in olive oil on medium heat for about 10 minutes, or until the meat is browned and cooked.

****

Quail Casserole

6 quartered quail breasts
1/4 cup of butter
1/2 cup of onion, diced
1/2 cup of celery, chopped
1 tbsp. of cornstarch
8 oz. of chicken broth
2 tbsp. of sherry
2 tbsp. of parsley, chopped
Salt and pepper to taste

Sauté the quail in the butter for about 10 minutes. Remove the meat and sauté the onion and celery in the remaining butter for about 5 minutes. Dissolve the cornstarch in the chicken broth and add it to the skillet. Simmer, stirring constantly until it begins to thicken, then stir in the sherry, parsley, salt, and pepper. Arrange the meat in a casserole dish sprayed with cooking spray, and pour the sauce over it. Preheat the oven to 350 degrees and bake the casserole for about 15 minutes.

Fried Venison Fingers

1 lb. of venison steak
1 cup of milk
1 cup of flour
2 eggs, beaten
1 stack of crushed crackers
Salt and pepper to taste

Cut the venison into strips about 1" long and 1/2" wide. Soak them in milk for about 5 minutes, then dip them in the flour, then the eggs and then the crackers. Salt and pepper to taste. Fry the strips on both sides until they are browned and cooked to your satisfaction.

****

Pheasant, Quail or Dove

3 to 4 lb. of cut up bird meat
Salt and pepper to taste
1/2 lb. of butter
1/2 cup of sherry
1/4 cup of chopped almonds
1 tbsp. of onion, minced
1 clove of garlic, minced
3 cups of chicken broth
3 tbsp. of flour

Salt and pepper the bird meat and brown it in a skillet in the butter. Add 1/4 cup of the sherry and simmer for about 2 minutes. Move the meat to a large casserole dish. Brown the almonds, onion, and garlic, then add the other 1/4 cup of sherry and the chicken broth. Stir in the flour to thicken the mixture, then pour it over the meat. Preheat the oven to 300 degrees and bake for about 2 hours.

Chili Rellenos Casserole

2 cans of whole green chilies
3 cups of sharp cheddar cheese, shredded
4 green onions
3 cups of Mozzarella cheese, shredded
6 eggs
1/4 to 1/2 cup milk
3/4 cups of flour
1/4 tsp. of salt
2 cans of green chili salsa

Split the whole chilies lengthwise and remove the seeds. Single layer them in a greased 9" x 13" pan. Sprinkle with shredded cheddar cheese, green onions, and 1 and 1/2 cups of mozzarella.

Beat the eggs, milk, flour, and salt until smooth. Pour over the chilies and cheese. Bake at 325 degrees for 50 minutes.

Meanwhile, mix the salsa with the remaining 1and 1/2 cups of mozzarella. Sprinkle over the casserole and return to the oven for an additional 10 minutes. Let stand for 5 minutes before serving.

Contributed by Patsy Lethgo

Eggplant Parmesan

Slice the eggplant into pieces about 1/4 to 1/2 inch in thickness. Beat 1 or 2 eggs in a bowl. Dip the eggplant slices in the egg to coat them. Coat the eggplant with Italian breadcrumbs.

Heat 3 tbsp. of olive oil and 3 tbsp. of butter in a large pan. Brown the eggplant on both sides. After browning, place the eggplant in a large, greased baking dish. Spread a light layer of Marinara sauce on each slice. Sprinkle a mixture of shredded Parmesan and mozzarella cheese on the slices.

Bake in the oven preheated to 350 degrees for 15 to 20 minutes until eggplant is tender.

Contributed by R. E. Armstrong

Asian Crab and Sauce

3 tbsp. of ketchup
Salt to taste
1 and 1/2 tsp. of sugar
1/2 tsp. of soy sauce
1 tsp. of soybean paste
1 and 1/2 tsp. of corn flour
1/2 tsp. of lime juice (or rice vinegar)
1 cup of water
1 to 2 tbsp. of cooking oil
3 cloves of garlic, minced
1/2 tsp. of ground red pepper (more or less depending on individual taste)
1/2 to 1 lb. of fresh or imitation crab, chunks

Completely mix the ketchup, salt, sugar, soy sauce, soybean paste, corn flour, lime juice, and water in a bowl. Stir well until the ingredients are blended. Put the oil in a skillet or wok and heat over medium heat. Sauté the garlic and ground red pepper for about 1 to 2 minutes, then stir in the crabmeat. Stir and simmer until the meat is cooked to your satisfaction. Use the sauce to dip the crabmeat in or put the crabmeat over cooked rice and top with some sauce.

SIDE DISHES

Baked Squash

2 or 3 zucchini squash, chopped into bite size pieces
2 or 3 yellow squash, chopped into bite size pieces
1 large yellow onion, chopped into bite size pieces
About 10 baby carrots, chopped into smaller pieces for faster cooking
Italian seasoning
Olive oil

    Combine the vegetables in a large zip lock bag. Sprinkle in enough dried Italian seasoning to lightly coat the vegetable pieces when the bag is shaken. Then pour in enough olive oil to coat all the vegetables when the bag is shaken again. Pour the vegetables into a baking dish sprayed with non-stick cooking spray. Bake at 400 degrees for 45 to 60 minutes, stirring as needed.

Contributed by R. E. Armstrong

Baked Eggplant and Tomato

1 large eggplant, sliced cross ways into 1/8" thick round slices
Sea salt and fresh ground black pepper to taste
2 tbsp. (or more) of olive oil
2 tomatoes, sliced like the eggplant
1 cup of basil, chopped
Feta or other favorite cheese, sliced thin
Olive oil
Fresh ground black pepper

Sprinkle the eggplant slices with sea salt and set aside for 20 to 30 minutes. Then rinse the eggplant slices and dry them with paper towels. Heat a little olive oil in a skillet and lightly fry the eggplant slices until they are slightly tender. In a baking dish, layer the eggplant slices, then top each one with a slice of tomato, a sprinkle of basil and a slice of your favorite cheese. Drizzle olive oil over the tops and fresh ground black pepper to taste. Bake them in an oven preheated to 350 degrees until the eggplant is tender.

Grilled Squash and Onion

2 tbsp. of olive oil
1/4 tsp. of cumin
Sea salt and fresh ground black pepper to taste
2 small yellow squash
2 small zucchini squash
1 red onion

In a large bowl, mix the olive oil, cumin, salt, and pepper. Cut both kinds of squash length ways and then cross ways into 1/2" thick pieces. Put the squash into the bowl and stir to coat each piece. Then using a slotted spoon move the squash to a grilling basket.

Cut the onion in fourths and place the pieces in the bowl stirring to coat each piece. Then using the slotted spoon move the onion to the grilling basket. Place the basket on the grill turning occasionally and grill for 10 to 15 minutes, or until done to your satisfaction.

Fettuccini Alfredo

2 lb. of Alfredo egg noodle pasta
12-16 oz. of fresh Parmesan cheese (not pre-grated in a can)
2 egg yokes
2 cups of heavy cream
1 stick of real butter

Cook the Alfredo noodles according to the directions on the package. Grate the cheese very fine and set aside. Combine the egg yokes with the cream, and whisk to blend together in a medium size pot. Add the butter, and heat on low to medium until the butter is melted and blended well.

Increase the heat to medium, and slowly add the grated cheese in small amounts while stirring. Continue to add the cheese, making sure each additional amount has melted and blended before adding more until all the cheese is used up. If you have done this properly you should end up with a semi thick creamy sauce. Pour the sauce over the pasta, and allow it to cool slightly to thicken. Stir and serve.

Contributed by Michael Bashta

Baked Apples and Sweet Potatoes

6 large sweet potatoes, peeled, sliced and boiled
1/2 cup of softened butter
6 apples, peeled and sliced
1/2 cup of brown sugar
Cinnamon

Spray a large casserole dish with non-stick cooking spray, and layer the sweet potatoes in it. Put a dot of softened butter on each potato slice and sprinkle with brown sugar and a little cinnamon. Then put a layer of apple slices on the potatoes and sprinkle with a little brown sugar and cinnamon. Continue layering, making the top layer be a layer of potato slices topped with butter, brown sugar, and cinnamon. Bake in the oven preheated to 350 degrees for about 30 to 45 minutes, or until the potatoes are brown and tender.

Contributed by T. J. McGinley

****

Ham and Navy Bean Soup

1 lb. of dry Navy beans, soaked overnight
1 lb. of lean boneless ham, cut into bite size pieces
1 and 1/2 quarts of water
3 cloves of garlic, minced
Salt and pepper to taste

Drain the soaked beans and discard the water. Then combine all the ingredients in a crock-pot (including the 1 and 1/2 quarts of fresh water) and cook on high heat for about 4 hours.

Contributed by Terry Rizzuti

Potatoes with Parsley Sauce

1 to 1 and 1/2 lb. of small new potatoes, washed
1 tbsp. of olive oil
1 clove of garlic, minced
1 medium onion, chopped
1 cup of chicken broth
1 cup of chopped parsley
Salt and pepper to taste

Cut the potatoes in half and put them in a bowl of cool water. Put the oil in a large skillet and heat over medium heat. Sauté the garlic and onions for about 3 to 5 minutes. Add the chicken broth and about 3/4 of the parsley, bringing it to a boil while mixing well. Add salt and pepper.

Place the potatoes in a single layer in the skillet. Return to a boil and reduce the heat. Cover the skillet and simmer until the potatoes are tender (about 10 minutes). Spoon the potatoes into a serving bowl and spoon the parsley sauce over the potatoes. Sprinkle the remaining parsley over the dish.

****

Baked Green Beans

1/4 lb. of bacon, cut into 1/2 inch strips
2 medium onions, diced
2 12-oz. cans of green beans, drained
1 can of tomato soup
1 can of water

Sauté the bacon and onions until cooked, then drain off the grease. Add the green beans and tomato soup and water. Mix well, then put into a casserole dish and bake in the oven preheated to 350 degrees. Cook until the mixture thickens, stirring occasionally to keep from overcooking the beans. Makes a good side dish for ham or turkey.

Contributed by George Horgan

Potato's Delicious

2 lb. of frozen hash browns, thawed
1/4 cup of diced onion
1 can of cream of chicken soup
1 pt. of cream
1/2 cup of sour cream
1/2 cup of butter, melted
1 tsp. of salt
Crackers, crushed

Layer the hash browns in a 9"x13" baking pan, then sprinkle the diced onions over the top. In a large bow, mix the chicken soup, cream, sour cream, melted butter, and salt. Blend these ingredients well then pour over the top of the hash browns and onions. Put 1 cup of crushed crackers on top and bake in a preheated oven at 350 degrees for 1 hour.

Contributed by Elsie Stromberg (In memory of her brother Verle N. Larson)

Mashed Potato Casserole

5 to 6 cups of mashed potatoes
8 oz. of sour cream
8 oz. of cream cheese
4 oz. of milk
1/4 tsp. of ground nutmeg
1 tsp. of garlic salt
2 tsp. of parsley flakes
10 slices of crisp cooked bacon
3/4 cup of cheddar cheese, shredded

Blend all of the ingredients (except the bacon and shredded cheese) in a large bowl using a mixer until smooth. Then place the mixture into a greased or sprayed baking dish or pan. Crumble up the bacon and sprinkle it and the shredded cheese over the top. Cover and bake in the oven preheated to 350 degrees for about 30 minutes.

Contributed by Terry Rizzuti

Garlic Mashed Potatoes

3 or 4 potatoes, washed, pealed and diced
3 cloves of garlic, minced
Salt and pepper to taste
3 tbsp. of butter
8 oz. of sour cream

Combine the potatoes, garlic, salt, and pepper in a pot, and add enough water to cover the potatoes. Bring to a boil, reduce the heat, stir and simmer until the potatoes are cooked enough for easy mashing. Pour off the excess water, and add the butter and sour cream to the potatoes. Mash with a potato masher, stirring until the potatoes and other ingredients become smooth and creamy. Serve as a side dish with steak or other favorite meats.

Contributed by R. E. Armstrong

****

Batter Fried Tomatoes

4 half ripe tomatoes
1/2 cup of flour
2 and 1/2 tsp. of sugar
Salt and pepper to taste
3/4 cup of evaporated milk
Olive oil

Wash the tomatoes and cut them into 1/2" thick slices. Combine the flour, sugar, salt, and pepper. Coat the tomato slices on both sides with the flour mixture. Add the milk to the remaining flour mixture to make a batter. Dip the floured tomatoes in the batter and fry them in hot olive oil until they are browned on both sides.

Spanish Potato Salad

Potato Salad:

8 medium red potatoes, steamed (or boiled) until tender, cooled and then sliced
1 stalk of celery, chopped
1/4 cup of onions, diced
2 cloves of garlic, minced
1/4 cup of diced bell pepper
1/2 cup of green olives stuffed with pimentos, sliced
1/4 cup of chopped parsley

Mix all the potato salad ingredients together in a large bowl.

Salad Dressing:

1/4 cup of fresh lemon juice
1/4 cup of olive oil
1/2 tsp. of dried thyme
1/4 tsp. of black pepper
1/2 tsp. of sea salt

Mix all the salad dressing ingredients and pour over the potato salad. Mix well and refrigerate.

Contributed by Diane Mercier

Stir Fried Rice and Onions

3 cups of long grain rice
1 tbsp. of soy sauce
White pepper to taste
1 and 1/2 tbsp. of oil
1/2 tsp. of chili oil
1/2 cup of green onions, chopped
1 egg, beaten
1/4 tsp. of sesame oil
1/4 cup of cilantro, minced

Combine the rice, soy sauce, and pepper in a large bowl. Cook according to rice directions. Heat the cooking oil and chili oil in a large skillet or wok until it is hot. Add the chopped onion and egg, then stir-fry for about 30 seconds. Then add the cooked rice and stir-fry for about 3 to 5 minutes or until it is heated and blended with the other ingredients. Stir in the sesame oil and cilantro and serve. *Cooked and diced ham can be added with the egg and onion for added flavor.*

Contributed by Terry Rizzuti

****

Fried Zucchini Fritters

2 medium size zucchini squash, grated
1 carrot, peeled and grated
Olive oil
1/2 cup of flour
Sea salt to taste (optional)
1 egg, beaten

Mix all of the ingredients together well. Heat enough olive oil in a skillet to fry with, and drop the zucchini mixture into the skillet using a tablespoon. Fry until the zucchini begins to turn brown, then remove from the skillet, drain the excess oil and serve.

Fat Albert's Potato Salad

8 or 9 medium red or white potatoes, peeled and quartered
1/2 cup of celery, diced
3/4 cup of dill pickles, diced
1/4 cup of olives, black or green, diced
1 bunch of green onions, diced
2 and 1/2 heaping tbsp. of mayonnaise
3/4 tsp. of salt
4 or 5 deviled eggs (optional)
Paprika

Boil the potatoes in a large pot until just barely done. Discard the water and refill the pot with cold water, completely covering the potatoes, and set aside until the potatoes are cool about 30 minutes. Meanwhile combine all the other ingredients, except the eggs and paprika, in a very large bowl and set aside. Add the cooled potatoes and mix well, very lightly mashing the potatoes as you do so. Arrange your favorite deviled eggs around the outside of the potato salad (optional), and lightly sprinkle paprika on top. Refrigerate for at least 4 hours before serving.

Contributed by Terry Rizzuti

Potato and Lettuce Salad

2 cups of diced potatoes, peeled and cooked
2 cups of lettuce, chopped
1 cup of cooked green beans, cut into bite size pieces
1 cup of cooked peas
1 large tomato, diced
1 hard boiled egg, sliced

   Mix the potatoes, lettuce, green beans, peas, and tomato together in a large bowl. Pour in some of your favorite vinaigrette (or other) dressing and toss the ingredients together. Top with slices of hard-boiled egg and serve.

Contributed by a member of the American Legion

****

Spicy Mexican Rice

1 cup of uncooked minute rice
2 tbsp. oil
1 bell pepper, diced
1 small onion. diced
28 oz. of canned tomatoes
Water (if needed)
1 tsp. of chili powder (optional)
1/2 tsp. of cayenne pepper (optional)

   Stir fry 3 tbsp. of the rice until it begins to turn brown in hot oil. Add the bell pepper and onion, and continue to fry for about 2 minutes. Then add the canned tomatoes, the rest of the rice (water if needed), the chili powder, and cayenne pepper (if desired). Cover and simmer for about 30 minutes.

Contributed by Shawn Flanagan

White Bean Salad

1 tsp. of red wine vinegar
1 tbsp. of olive oil
Sea salt and fresh ground black pepper to taste
1 can of white beans (about 16 oz), drained and rinsed
1 tomato, diced
3 or 4 green onions, diced

In a bowl, combine the red wine vinegar, olive oil, sea salt, and fresh ground black pepper. Blend well then add the white beans, tomatoes, and diced onions. Stir the ingredients until they are well mixed.

Contributed by Terry Rizzuti

****

Parmesan Potatoes

1 to 2 lb. of small red potatoes
3 tbsp. of olive oil
Sea salt and black pepper to taste
2 tbsp. of grated Parmesan cheese

Cut the potatoes into bite size chunks and put them in a re-sealable plastic bag or a container with a cover. Add the olive oil, seal and toss or shake the potatoes until they are coated by the olive oil.

In a baking dish or pan, spread the potatoes out in a single layer and sprinkle with sea salt and fresh ground black pepper to taste. Bake the potatoes in an oven preheated to 425 degrees for about 20 minutes, turn the potatoes and sprinkle the cheese over them. Bake for about 20 more minutes or until the potatoes are tender.

Contributed by T. J. McGinley

Fried Bell Peppers

1 to 2 lb. of bell peppers
2 tbsp. of olive oil
1 tbsp. of balsamic vinegar
Sea salt and black pepper to taste

Cut the bell peppers into strips about 1/2 inch wide, removing the seeds and ribs. Heat the olive oil in a large skillet and cook the peppers (stirring often) for about 5 to 10 minutes until they are softened. Remove the skillet from the heat and add the balsamic vinegar while stirring the peppers. Add sea salt and fresh ground black pepper to taste.

Contributed by Phil Huston

****

Spicy Rice

1/2 cup of green onions, diced
1/2 cup of baby carrots, diced
1 bell pepper, diced
1 tbsp. of olive oil
2 cups of rice, cooked in chicken broth
1 tbsp. of cilantro, chopped
1 tbsp. of lime juice
1 tsp. of soy sauce
1 jalapeno pepper, minced
Hot pepper sauce to taste

In a large skillet, sauté the onions, carrots, bell pepper, and jalapeno pepper in olive oil over medium heat until tender. Then stir in the cooked rice, cilantro, lime juice, soy sauce, and pepper sauces. Stirring frequently, cook until everything is well heated.

Contributed by Terry Rizzuti

Garbanzo Bean Salad

1 cup of cooked garbanzo beans
1 bell pepper, diced
1 small red onion, sliced thin
2 small cucumbers, peeled and sliced thin
Sea salt and fresh ground black pepper to taste

Stir all the ingredients together in a large bowl and sprinkle with your favorite dressing (vinaigrette goes well with this). Stir the salad well, then cover and refrigerate for about 2 hours. Stir the salad again just before serving to keep the dressing from staying at the bottom of the bowl.

Contributed by Brian Young

****

Cucumber and Mushroom Salad

2 cups of cucumber, sliced thin
3 cups of fresh mushrooms, sliced
1/3 cup of green onions, sliced
1 small bell pepper, diced
1/2 cup of white wine vinegar
1/4 cup of sugar
Sea salt and fresh ground black pepper to taste
1 tbsp. of chopped fresh dill

Combine the cucumber, mushrooms, green onions, and diced bell pepper in a large bowl and stir well. In another bowl, combine the vinegar, sugar, sea salt, black pepper, and chopped dill, stirring until the sugar is completely dissolved, then pour over the salad mixture. Stir the salad to coat all the mix, then cover and refrigerate for at least 2 hours, stirring occasionally.

Contributed by Shawn Flanagan

Stir Fried Broccoli

2 lb. of fresh broccoli
2 cloves of garlic, minced
1/2 cup of water
1/4 cup of olive oil
Salt and pepper to taste

Wash the broccoli, then split the stalks lengthwise then crosswise to make them bite size. Put the broccoli in a large skillet and sprinkle it with the garlic, water, and olive oil. Salt and pepper to taste. Cover the skillet and cook over low heat for about 20 to 30 minutes until the broccoli is tender. Stir several times during cooking.

****

Baked Eggplant

1 small onion, diced
2 tbsp. of olive oil
10 oz. of tomato puree
2/3 cup of water
Salt and pepper to taste
1 tsp. of oregano
1 eggplant, peeled and sliced thin
1 can of tomato sauce
2 cups of shredded Parmesan or cheddar cheese

In a skillet, sauté the diced onions in the olive oil. Add the tomato puree, water, salt, pepper, and oregano. Bring to a boil and simmer for about 15 minutes to make a tomato sauce. In a greased baking dish alternate layers of eggplant, tomato sauce and 1 cup of the cheese, beginning with a layer of eggplant and ending with a layer of tomato sauce. Preheat the oven to 350 degrees and bake the eggplant for about 60 minutes. Before removing it from the oven, sprinkle the remaining cheese over the top and continue heating until the cheese melts.

Candied Sweet Potatoes

1 cup of dark Karo corn syrup
1/2 cup of dark brown sugar
2 tbsp. of butter
12 sweet potatoes, cooked and peeled, cut in half lengthwise

In a pot, combine the corn syrup, brown sugar, and butter. Heat until it boils, then lower the heat and simmer for about 5 minutes. Pour half of the syrup mix into a 9"x13" baking dish. Arrange the potatoes in the dish, and pour the remaining syrup over them. Bake the potatoes in a preheated oven at 350 degrees for about 20 minutes, basting often until they are well glazed.

****

German Potato Salad

2 lb. of potatoes
1/4 lb of bacon, cut into small pieces
1 small onion, diced
1/4 cup of water
1/2 cup of cider vinegar
4 tsp. of sugar
Salt to taste
1 tsp. of mustard
1 tsp. of mustard seeds
2 tbsp. of parsley
1 tsp. of paprika

Wash the potatoes and boil them in salted water. When the potatoes are tender, drain them and let them cool. When cooled, peel the potatoes and slice them cross wise about 1/4" thick. Fry the bacon until it is crisp, then remove it from the pan and pour off all of the grease except for 2 to 3 tbsp. Sauté the diced onion in the grease until it is tender. In a large bowl, combine the water, vinegar, sugar, salt, mustard, and mustard seeds. Add the potato slices and toss well until they are all coated. Sprinkle with the crispy bacon, parsley, and paprika.

Tuna Casserole

1 10-oz. can of mushroom soup
1/4 cup of milk
1 7-oz. can of chunk white tuna, drained and flaked
2 sliced hard boiled eggs
1 cup of cooked peas
Potato chips, crumbled

In a casserole dish, blend the mushroom soup and milk, then stir in the tuna, sliced eggs, and cooked peas. In a preheated oven bake the casserole at 350 degrees 30 to 45 minutes or until it is hot. Top with crumbled potato chips (optional).

****

Salmon Loaf

1 16-oz. can of salmon, drained and flaked
1/2 cup of dry bread crumbs
Salt to taste
1/2 cup of mayonnaise
1 small onion, diced
1 egg, beaten
1/4 cup of bell pepper, diced
1/4 cup of celery, chopped

Combine all the ingredients well, then shape into a loaf in a shallow baking dish. Preheat the oven to 350 degrees and bake the salmon loaf for about 40 to 45 minutes or until done.

Italian Bean Soup

1 bell pepper, chopped
1 tbsp. of olive oil
2 14-oz. cans of beef broth
1 15-oz. can of cannelloni beans, drained and rinsed
1 15-oz. can of kidney beans, drained and rinsed
2 14-oz. cans of diced tomatoes
1 cup of sliced carrots
1/2 onion, diced
2 cloves of garlic, minced
1 tsp. of Italian seasoning
Salt to taste
Hot sauce to taste
1 cup of uncooked elbow macaroni
Shredded Parmesan cheese

In a large pot, sauté the chopped bell pepper in the olive oil until it is tender. Add the beef broth and all of the other ingredients except for the elbow macaroni and Parmesan cheese. Bring the mixture to a boil then lower the heat, cover the pot and simmer, stirring occasionally for about 20 minutes. Add the macaroni and cover the pot again. Simmer the mixture for another 15 to 20 minutes or until the macaroni is cooked. Serve in bowls and sprinkle with Parmesan cheese.

Meatballs

2 slices of white sandwich bread torn into small cubes, crust discarded
1/2 cup of buttermilk
1 lb. ground chuck, or 3/4 lb. mixed with 1/4 lb. ground pork
1/4 cup of Parmesan cheese, freshly grated
2 tbsp. fresh parsley, minced
1 large egg yolk
1 garlic clove, minced
3/4 tsp. salt
Ground black pepper to taste
1 and 1/4 cups of vegetable oil for frying

Combine the bread and buttermilk in a small bowl, mashing with a fork until a smooth paste forms, about 10 minutes. Mix all the ingredients, including the bread mixture, in a large size bowl. Lightly form into 1 and 1/2 inch meatballs (approximately 14 meatballs).

Heat the vegetable oil over a medium high heat in a 10" or 11" sauté or frying pan until the edge of one "test" meatball dipped in the oil sizzles, then add the remaining meatballs. Fry, turning the meatballs several times until they are nicely browned (about 10 minutes), regulating the heat so the oil sizzles but doesn't smoke. Remove, drain on paper towels, and serve with your favorite pasta dish.

This was my mother's recipe. I frequently add onion flakes, oregano, and basil. Also, to reduce the grease, rather than fry them I bake the meatballs in the oven at 350 degrees for approximately 30 to 45 minutes. I also double the recipe and freeze half the meatballs in freezer bags for later use in a quick spaghetti meal.

Contributed by Terry Rizzuti (in memory of Teresa "Tess" Rizzuti)

Stir Fried Spinach

In a large pan or pot, heat 2 or 3 tsp. of olive oil. Sauté 2 or 3 cloves of minced garlic in the oil. Stir in about 1 lb. of clean, fresh spinach, and cook until the spinach begins to wilt. Add sea salt and fresh ground black pepper to taste. Serve warm with a bottle of vinegar pepper sauce to sprinkle on the spinach.

Contributed by R. E. Armstrong

****

Vegetable Bake

1/4 stick of butter, melted
2 tsp. of thyme, chopped
3/4 lb. of potatoes, thin sliced
Salt and pepper to taste
2 each yellow and zucchini squash, sliced thin
1 cup of tomato sauce
1/2 cup of grated Parmesan cheese

Mix the butter and thyme and coat the potatoes with 1/2 of the mix. Salt and pepper and place in a greased pan. Coat the squash with the other half of the butter/thyme mix, then salt and pepper. Layer the squash on the potatoes and spread the tomato sauce over all, cover with foil, and bake at 350 degrees for 45 minutes. Remove the foil. Top with cheese. Bake 10 minutes longer.

Contributed by Terry Rizzuti

Potato Pancakes

4 large potatoes, peeled and grated fine
1/4 cup of onion, finely grated
1 egg, beaten
2 tbsp. of flour
Sea salt and ground pepper to taste

Mix all of the ingredients in a large bowl. Spoon the ingredients into a skillet lightly oiled with olive oil and cook like you would pancakes. Serve warm with applesauce or sour cream for a topping.
Note: For added flavor, try adding crisp crumbled bacon or diced cooked ham to the ingredients before cooking.

Contributed by R. E. Armstrong

****

Tater-Tot Casserole

2 and 1/2 lb. of lean ground beef (seasoned with your favorite meat loaf seasonings)
1 can of cream soup of choice
1 package of frozen tater tots
1 cup of shredded cheese of choice

Put the meat mixture into a 9"x 13" baking pan. Spread the can of cream soup over the top of the meat mixture. Layer the tater tots evenly over the soup. Sprinkle with cheese. Bake at 350 degrees for 45 minutes to 1 hour.

Contributed by Patsy Lethgo

Bubba's Baked Beans

2 slices of bacon
30 oz. of pork and beans
1 cup of ketchup
1 tbsp. of mustard
2 tbsp. of brown sugar
1 small onion, diced

Brown the bacon slices in a small skillet. Mix the other ingredients in a large bowl, stirring well. Crumble the bacon slices into the bean mixture, and add the small amount of bacon grease from the skillet for flavoring. Mix all of the ingredients well and put them into a large baking dish. Preheat the oven to 350 degrees, and bake the beans for about 1 hour.

Contributed by R. E. Armstrong

Three Bean Casserole

1/2 lb. of bacon	1 medium onion, chopped
1/2 lb. of hamburger	1/4 lb. of smoked sausage
2 16-oz. cans of pork and beans	1 16-oz. can of kidney beans
1 16-oz. can of butter beans	1 tsp. of liquid smoke
1/4 cup of ketchup	1/3 cup of brown sugar
1/3 cup of white sugar	1/2 tsp. of salt
1/2 tsp. of pepper	1 tbsp. of dry mustard

Cut the bacon strips into fourths and cook until not quite crispy. Then add the onion, hamburger, and sausage. Cook until the hamburger is brown. Then drain the grease from the meats. In a bowl, mix the sugars, ketchup, liquid smoke, dry mustard, salt, and pepper to make a sauce. Pour the sauce into the meat and mix well. Drain the juice from the kidney and butter beans. In a large bowl, mix the pork and beans, kidney beans, and butter beans. Then mix with the meat and sauce mixture. Pour into a baking dish and bake covered at 350 degrees for 1 hour.

Contributed by Homer and Sue Aebi

****

Sausage Gravy

1/2 lb. of pork sausage
3 tbsp. of flour
2 cups of milk

In a frying pan, brown the sausage, leaving the grease in it. Add the flour and mix it well. Add the milk and stir constantly until it thickens. Remove from the heat, and serve the sausage gravy over split biscuits. Salt and pepper to taste.

Contributed by Stella Cichonski

SOUPS, SALADS AND SANDWICHES

Oriental Slaw Salad

1 lb. bag of slaw mix or shredded cabbage
1 bunch of cut up green onions
2/3 cup of oil
1/2 cup of sugar
2/3 cup of vinegar
2 packages of Ramen noodles, Oriental flavor
1 cup of sunflower seeds

Mix the slaw/shredded cabbage and onions. For the dressing, shake the oil, sugar, vinegar, and the two flavor packets from the Ramen noodles in a jar. Just before serving, crush the noodles and sprinkle in the salad with the sunflower seeds. Toss in the dressing.

Contributed by Imelda Armstrong

Teriyaki Sandwiches

2 lbs. of boneless chuck steak	2 tbsp. of water
1/4 cup of soy sauce	8 French rolls, split
1 tbsp. of brown sugar	1/4 cup of butter, melted
1 tsp. of ground ginger	Pineapple rings
1 garlic clove, minced	Green onions, Chopped
4 tsp. of cornstarch	

Cut the steak into thin bite-size slices. In a crock-pot, combine the soy sauce, sugar, ginger, and garlic. Add the steak. Cover and cook on low heat for 7 to 9 hours. Remove the meat with a slotted spoon and set aside.

Carefully pour the liquid into a 2-cup measuring cup; skim the fat. Add water to the liquid to measure 1 and 1/2 cups. Pour into a saucepan. Combine the cornstarch and water until smooth; add to pan.

Cook and stir until thick and bubbly, about 2 minutes. Add the meat to the pan and heat through. Brush the rolls with butter, and broil until browned slightly. Fill with meat, pineapple and green onions. *Makes about 8 servings.*

Contributed by Patsy Lethgo

Cambodian Salad

1 cabbage, finely shredded
1 small package of rice noodles
1/3 lb. of cooked pork, shredded
1 bunch of scallions
1 jar of crushed dry roasted peanuts

Combine all the salad ingredients in a large bowl and mix well.

Salad Sauce:

1 cup of fish sauce
1 cup of vinegar
1 cup of water
1 cup of sugar
5 cloves of garlic, minced

Completely mix the sauce ingredients and pour over the salad.

Contributed by Terry Rizzuti

Wally's In-Between-Wives Turkey Salad

1 head of iceberg lettuce, or equivalent amount of other types of lettuce
1/2 lb. of cold (cooked) turkey, crumbled or diced
1 can of unsalted cut green beans, drained
Salad dressing
Optional ingredients: Shredded carrots, radishes, artichoke hearts, black olives, croutons, imitation bacon bits, Mandarin oranges, etc.

Cut up or shred the lettuce to taste. Add the turkey and green beans and toss. Add your favorite salad dressing to taste. *Note: If the head of lettuce is especially solid, half of the head should do.*

Contributed by Walter Waldau

****

Cheesy Italian Bread

1 loaf of Italian bread
1 stick of real butter
3 cloves of garlic, minced
1 tbsp. of basil
Sharp cheddar cheese, grated

Slice the Italian bread lengthwise, then score both halves almost through at about 2 inch intervals. Heat the butter, garlic and basil in a small pan on low heat. Let the mixture sit for a while so the butter absorbs the flavor from the garlic and basil. Place the bread halves under the broiler long enough to toast the topside. Then spoon the butter mixture evenly over each piece. Sprinkle both halves of the bread with grated or shredded sharp cheddar cheese and place back under the broiler until the cheese melts.

Contributed by Terry Rizzuti

Bubba's Tater Soup

2 or 3 potatoes, peeled and chopped into bite size pieces
3 cloves of garlic, minced
3 tbsp. of butter
1 large yellow onion, diced
Sea salt and fresh ground black pepper to taste
1 to 2 cups of shredded cabbage (coleslaw mix)
3 or 4 slices of bacon

Place all the ingredients (except bacon) in a large pot and add enough water to cover all ingredients. Bring to a boil, then turn the heat down and simmer for 2 to 3 hours adding water as needed. Microwave 3 or 4 slices of your favorite bacon, crumble into the soup about 10 minutes before removing from the stove. Serve with cornbread or other fresh cooked bread.

Contributed by R. E. Armstrong

Pizza Cheese Bread

2 cans of Pillsbury biscuits
1/2 cup of sundried tomatoes
1/4 tsp. of garlic powder
1/4 tsp. of salt
1/4 tsp. of oregano
1/4 tsp. of basil
1/2 cup of Mozzarella cheese
1/2 cup of Parmesan cheese

Cut the biscuits into forths, and roll into balls. Place on a cookie sheet (with edges) and make sure that the balls are sticking together in some way. Pour the oil from the dried tomatoes on the bread. Then put on the sundried tomatoes. Mix the seasonings in a separate bowl and spread on the bread evenly. Sprinkle on the Mozzarella cheese and Parmesan cheese. Preheat the oven to 350 degrees, and bake for 10 minutes or until golden brown and crunchy.

Contributed by Patsy Lethgo

Cucumber Soup

1 tbsp. of olive oil
1 lb. of small cucumbers, peeled and diced
1 onion, diced
1 bell pepper, diced
3 cups of chicken broth
Sea salt and fresh ground black pepper to taste
Sour cream (or yogurt)
1 tbsp. of parsley

Warm the olive (or vegetable) oil in a pan over medium heat and sauté the cucumber, onion, and bell pepper about 10 to 15 minutes or until the vegetables are tender. Stir in the chicken broth and simmer for about 10 to 15 minutes more, stirring occasionally.

Then pour the mixture into a blender and puree until it is smooth, then pour it back into the pan. Bring it back to a low boil (simmer) and season it to your taste with sea salt and fresh ground black pepper. Serve the cucumber soup hot, and top it with some sour cream or yogurt and a sprinkle of parsley.

Contributed by R. E. Armstrong

Black Bean Soup

3 15-oz. cans of black beans, un-drained
2 cups of water
2 14-oz. cans of beef broth
1 1/2 cups of onion, diced
1 bell pepper, diced
3 cloves of garlic, minced
1 14-oz. can of diced tomatoes, no salt added
1 small can of chopped green chilies, un-drained
1/4 lb. of cooked ham, diced
1 tsp. of oregano
1/2 cup of red wine vinegar
1 tsp. of thyme
1 tsp. of cumin
Sea salt and ground black pepper to taste

Combine the black beans, water, beef broth, diced onion, bell pepper, and minced garlic in a large pot. Bring the mixture to a boil, then reduce the heat, cover and simmer for about 20 minutes, stirring frequently. Then stir in the remaining ingredients and cook uncovered for about 30 minutes more, stirring occasionally.

Contributed by Andy Hicks

Hot Roast Beef Sandwich

6 sandwich rolls
Softened butter
Garlic powder
Mozzarella cheese
1 can of beef broth
1 lb. of cooked roast beef, sliced thin

Slice the sandwich rolls down the center and lay open. Spread the softened butter on both sides then sprinkle with garlic powder. Place the Mozzarella cheese on both sides of the roll. Place under a broiler until the cheese melts. Heat the beef broth until it simmers, then dip the slices of roast beef in it until they are heated. Place the slices of heated roast beef on one side of the sandwich roll then close the roll around it. Serve the sandwiches with a bowl of the heated beef broth for dipping.

****

Santa Fe Soup

1 can of whole kernel corn
1 can of ranch style beans
1 can of Rotel
1 can of diced tomatoes
1 lb. of Velveeta cheese
1 lb. of browned hamburger or sausage, browned
Dorito chips

Empty all cans, including liquids, into a pot. Then add the Velveeta and browned meat. Heat until the cheese is melted. Serve over Doritos in a bowl.

Contributed by Homer and Sue Aebi

Middle Eastern Bread

6 cups of flour
1 tbsp. of salt
2 tbsp. plus 1 tsp. of sugar
2 and 1/2 cups of warm water
2 packages of yeast

Mix the flour, salt, and 2 tbsp. of sugar in a bowl. In another small bowl, mix 1/2 cup of water, the yeast packages and 1 tsp. of sugar. Add the mixture to the bowl with the flour mixture, then add the remainder of the warm water. Knead the dough and let it rise.

Divide the dough into balls and let stand for about 10 minutes. Roll the dough balls into 4 inch round shapes and place on a baking sheet. Bake in an oven pre-heated to 450 degrees for about 8 minutes. When cool, slice open one side and fill with whatever you like.

****

Tropical Salad

1/4 cup of shredded coconut
10 oz. of lettuce
1 8-oz. can of pineapple chunks (save the juice)
1 mango peeled, pitted and diced
1 cup of seedless grapes
1 to 2 cups of turkey, cooked and diced
1/4 cup of honey mustard
1/4 cup of sliced roasted almonds

Preheat the oven to 350 degrees and toast the coconut on a cookie sheet or shallow pan for about 5 minutes, stirring once or twice. In a large bowl, toss together the lettuce, pineapple, mango, and grapes. Then sprinkle the cooked turkey over the mixture. Stir the honey mustard and pineapple juice together and sprinkle over the salad. Then sprinkle the toasted coconut and almonds over the salad and serve.

Grilled Italian Turkey Sandwich

Ingredients needed for each sandwich:

2 thick slices of Italian or sourdough bread
Melted butter or olive oil
1 slice each of Provolone and Mozzarella cheese
2 slices of smoked turkey or chicken, sliced thick (1/8 inch or more)
Sliced black olives
Roasted peppers
Italian dressing or spicy mustard

Brush each slice of bread with melted butter or olive oil on both sides. Lightly brown one side of bread in a skillet or on a grill. Turn the bread over and layer one slice with a piece of cheese, turkey, cheese, and turkey, in that order. Place a layer of sliced olives over the last layer of turkey, then a layer of roasted peppers. Drizzle the ingredients with either Italian dressing or spicy brown mustard. Top with the other slice of bread and enjoy.

Contributed by R. E. Armstrong

DESSERTS

Tomato Soup Cake

2 cups of flour
2 tsp. of baking powder
1 tsp. of cinnamon
1 tsp. of nutmeg
1/2 tsp. of ground cloves
2 eggs or 4 oz. of egg substitute
3/4 cup of sugar
1 can (10 and 3/4 ounces) of tomato soup
1/2 cup of walnuts, chopped

Sift the flour, baking powder, cinnamon, nutmeg, and cloves together and set aside. Combine the eggs, sugar, and tomato soup. Gradually add the flour mixture to the liquid mixture. Stir in the walnuts. Pour into a Bundt pan that has been sprayed with nonstick spray. Preheat the oven to 350 degrees and bake for 25 to 30 minutes.

Contributed by Patsy Lethgo

Chocolate Glaze

6 oz. of high quality semi-sweet chocolate, finely chopped
3/4 cup of heavy cream

Place the chopped chocolate in a bowl. Scald the cream. Pour the hot cream over the chocolate and gently stir to melt all the chocolate.

This can be made up to 3 days before and reheated slightly for use. The glaze should be drizzled over cakes, cookies, etc. when it's at room temperature, or slightly warm, but still liquid. If the glaze is hot, it will drip too much.

Yield: About 1 1/3 cups   Prep Time: 5 minutes   Cooking Time: 5 minutes

Contributed by Patsy Lethgo

Peanut Butter Pie

Pie Filling:

2 cups of creamy peanut butter
1 and 3/4 cups of sugar
16 oz of cream cheese, warmed to room temperature
1 cup of heavy whipping cream
1 graham cracker pie crust

In a large bowl, blend the peanut butter, sugar, and cream cheese. Mix until the ingredients are completely blended. In another bowl, whip the heavy cream with a mixer until the cream becomes stiff, then stir it into the peanut butter mixture. Spoon the mixture into a cooled graham cracker pie crust.

Pie Topping:

2/3 cup of heavy whipping cream
1/3 cup of sugar
3 oz, of semisweet chocolate
1/2 cup of butter
1 tsp. of vanilla extract
Roasted Peanuts, chopped (optional)

Put the whipping cream and sugar in a pot or pan and bring it to a boil, then reduce the heat and simmer it for 6 to 8 minutes. Remove it from the heat and add the chocolate and butter, stirring until they are melted. Stir in the vanilla and let cool until it begins to thicken, then pour it evenly over the pie. Refrigerate the pie for 4 to 6 hours before serving. Pie can be topped with a sprinkle of chopped roasted peanuts for added flavor.

Contributed by T. J. McGinley

Deluxe Lemon Cake

1 package lemon cake mix
3 tbsp. of flour
2/3 cup of oil
1 package of lemon instant pudding
1 1/3 cup of water
4 Eggs

Combine all the above ingredients together and beat for 4 minutes. Bake at 350 degrees for about 40 minutes. When hot, punch holes all over the cake with a fork.

Mix and pour the following over the top of the hot cake:

2 cups powdered sugar
1 frozen lemon aide

Contributed by Patsy Lethgo

Patsy's Divinity Candy

4 cups of granulated sugar
3/4 cup of water
1 cup of Kayo Syrup
3 egg whites, stiffly beaten
1 tsp. of vanilla
1 cup of nuts and any other fruits or chopped up candy canes, etc.

Place the first three ingredients in a saucepan over medium heat. Place candy thermometer on the side of the pan. Stir until the sugar is dissolved. Cook without stirring to 255 degrees. Remove from heat, and pour into stiff egg whites, beating constantly until thick and the gloss is gone. Add the vanilla and nuts. Place in a greased pan, or drop onto waxed paper using a tablespoon. Allow to set until very dry. Cut into pieces and enjoy!

Contributed by Patsy Lethgo

****

Ga-Ga's "Garbage Cookies"

1 egg
2 cups of flour
1 cup of granulated sugar
3/4 cup of shortening
1/4 cup of molasses
2 tsp. of baking Soda
1 tbsp. of cinnamon
1 tsp. of ginger
1 tsp. of vanilla
1/4 tsp. of salt

Mix all the ingredients and drop onto an un-greased cookie sheet. Bake at 375 degrees for about 10 min.

Contributed by Patsy Lethgo

Butterscotch Pudding

Especially liked by children.

3/4 cup of Karo, Blue Label
2 and 1/4 cups of milk
1/2 tbsp. of butter
1/3 tsp. of salt
1 tbsp. of Argo or Kingsford's Cornstarch
6 drops of vanilla

Scald the Karo and milk. Add the butter, salt, and cornstarch dissolved in an equal quantity of cold milk. Cook in a double boiler, stirring constantly until thickened, allowing twenty minutes. Add the vanilla, and chill, mold, and serve with sweetened cream.

Contributed by Patsy Lethgo

Peach Bread

1 and 1/2 cups of sugar
1/2 cup of shortening
2 eggs
2 and 1/4 cups of pureed peaches
1 tsp. of cinnamon
2 cups of all-purpose flour
1 tsp. of baking soda
1/4 tsp. of salt
1 tsp. of vanilla
1 cup of finely chopped pecans

Cream the sugar and shortening together. Add the eggs, and mix thoroughly. Add the peach puree and dry ingredients. Mix thoroughly. Add the vanilla and chopped pecans, and stir until blended.

Pour into two separate loaf pans approximately 5" x 9" in size, that have been well greased and floured. Bake at 325 degrees for 55 minutes to 1 hour. Let bread cool a few minutes before removing from pan. Makes 2 loaves.

Contributed by Patsy Lethgo

Cheese Cake

1 cup of graham cracker crumbs
1/4 cup plus 2 tbsp. of melted butter
2 eggs
1 lb. of cream cheese cut in small pieces

3/4 cup of sugar
1 and 1/2 cups of sour cream
2 tsp. of vanilla

Blend the cracker crumbs with 1/4 cup of the sugar and 1/4 cup of the melted butter, and line the bottom and sides of an 8 or 9-inch un-greased pan. Blend the sour cream, 1/2 cup of sugar, the eggs, and vanilla in a food blender for 1 minute. Add the cream cheese and blend until smooth. Blend in the remaining 2 tbsp. of melted butter. Pour the mixture into the baking pan. Bake in the lower third of the oven, preheated to 325 degrees for 45 minutes.

When the baking is done, remove the cake from the oven and turn the oven to broil. Broil the cheesecake just until the top begins to show attractive brown spots. Refrigerate for at least 4 hours or preferably overnight before cutting and serving. This is not a low calorie version, so cut into small pieces.

Contributed by Michael Bashta

Baked Apple Squares

1 can (21 oz.) of apple pie filling
1 egg
1/2 cup of sugar
1 tsp. of baking soda
1/2 tsp. of salt
1/2 tsp. of cinnamon
8 oz. of sour cream
1/4 cup of brown sugar, packed
1/2 cup of butter
2 cups of all-purpose flour

Combine all the ingredients in a bowl and mix well. Pour the mixture into a buttered 9"x13" baking dish or pan. Spread the ingredients so the thickness is even. Bake in the oven preheated to 350 degrees until the apples are tender. Cut into squares and serve.

****

Hawaiian Pineapple Candy

1 cup of granulated sugar
1/2 cup of brown sugar
1/4 cup of milk or cream
1/2 cup of crushed pineapple, not drained
1 tbsp. of butter
1 tsp. of vanilla
1/2 cup of pecans

Cook the sugars, milk, and pineapple until a thermometer reaches "soft ball" stage. Remove from heat. Add the butter, vanilla and nuts. Beat until creamy (the color will change as it gets stiff). If it is too stiff to drop from a spoon, add one spoonful of hot water at a timer as needed, being sure to beat after each addition of water.

Contributed by Patsy Lethgo

Mississippi Mud Cake

2 cups of sugar
1/4 tsp. of salt
1 cup of shortening
1 tsp. of vanilla
4 eggs
1 cup of nuts
1 and 1/2 cups of flour
1/2 package of mini marshmallows
1/3 cup of cocoa

Mix all the ingredients. Pour into a 9"x13" greased pan. Bake at 300 degrees for 35 minutes. Remove from the oven and pour Marshmallows over the top. Return to the oven for 10 min. at 350 degrees. Cool for 1 hour.

Icing for Mississippi Mud Cake:

1 lb. of powdered sugar
1/3 cup of cocoa
2 sticks of butter, melted
1 cup of nuts
1 tsp. of vanilla
1/3 cup of evaporated milk

Stir the sugar and cocoa. Mix with melted Butter. Add the nuts, vanilla, and milk. Spread on cake. Freezes very well.

Contributed by Patsy Lethgo

Blueberry Bundt Cake

1 Butter cake mix
8 oz. of cream cheese
1 cup of oil
3 eggs
1 cup of blueberries

Mix the cake mix, cream cheese, and oil in a large mixing bowl. Whip in the eggs 1 at a time. Fold in the blueberries. Bake in a Bundt cake pan at 350 degrees for 50 minutes.

Contributed by Imelda Armstrong

****

Mom's Chocolate Pie

Mix together 3/4 cups of sugar, 1/4 tsp. of salt, 3 tbsp. of cornstarch, and 3 tbsp. of cocoa. Add 1/4 cup of evaporated milk. Mix to a paste then add 1 and 3/4 cups of milk and cook until thick.

Add 3 egg yolks and 2 tbsp. of milk, then cook for 2 minutes. Add 4 tbsp. of Butter and 2 tsp. of vanilla. Mix until smooth, then pour into a baked pie shell and top with Meringue.

Contributed by Patsy Lethgo

Lemon Tarts

1 package of frozen pastry shells
4 eggs
1 and 1/4 cups of confection sugar
1 cup of lemon juice
2/3 cup of sour cream
1 lemon peel, grated

Bake the pastry shells according to the directions on the package. Lower the oven heat to 275 degrees. In a bowl, beat together the eggs, sugar, and lemon juice. Pour the sour cream and grated lemon peel into a small pan and warm it, then stir it into the egg mixture. Pour this filling into the pre-baked pastry shells and bake about 30 to 35 minutes or until the filling is set. Remove from the oven and cool. Refrigerate for several hours before serving.

Patsy's Pumpkin Cookies

2 cups of sugar
4 cups of flour
1 cup of oil
2 tsp. of baking powder
1 can of pumpkin (small can)
1 tsp. of salt
1 cup of nuts
2 tsp. of baking soda
1 cup of raisins
4 tbsp. of cinnamon
1/4 cup of molasses
1/2 tsp. of nutmeg
1 tbsp. of vanilla
1/2 tsp. of ground ginger

Mix all the ingredients in a mixer bowl. Drop by teaspoon onto a lightly greased cookie sheet about 2" apart. Bake at 375 degrees for 12 minutes. *Yields 7 to 8 dozen cookies.*

Contributed by Patsy Lethgo

Pumpkin Cheesecake

1 cream cheese (8 oz. low-calorie or fat-free)
1 can of pumpkin (16 oz. can)
1/2 cup of brown sugar
1 tsp. of vanilla
1 and 1/2 tsp. of pumpkin pie spices
2 eggs
1 8" graham cracker crust
2 cups of cool whip

Soften the cream cheese to room temperature, about 30 seconds in a microwave. Thoroughly combine the cream cheese, 3/4 of the can of pumpkin, brown sugar, vanilla, and spices. Slowly add the eggs to the mixture. Beat well. Pour into crust. Bake at 350 degrees for about 30 to 40 minutes or until the center is set. Cool on rack for one hour. Blend together the remaining 1/4 can pumpkin and cool whip. Spoon on top of pie. Chill for several hours.

Contributed by Patsy Lethgo

****

Pineapple Pie

1 14-oz. can of sweet condensed milk
1/2 cup of lemon juice
1 20-oz. can of crushed pineapple, drained
8 oz. of cool whip
1 baked graham cracker crust

In a bowl, mix the milk and lemon juice, and stir well. Stir in the crushed pineapple and cool whip. Spoon the mixture into the graham cracker pie crust and refrigerate for at least 2 hours.

Contributed by Christy Floyd

Strawberry Chiffon Pie

1 (4-serving-size) package of strawberry Jell-O
1/2 cup of hot water
1/4 cup of sugar
1 cup of evaporated milk (see note)
1/4 cup of fresh lemon juice
1and 1/2 cups of sliced fresh strawberries
1 baked 9-inch pie shell

Dissolve the gelatin in hot water, and add the sugar. Mix well and chill until thickened and syrupy. Whip the chilled milk until stiff, about 1 minute. Add the lemon juice and continue whipping until very stiff. Fold in the thickened gelatin and strawberries. Pour the filling into the pie shell. Chill until firm.

Note: To whip the evaporated milk, open the can and chill in the freezer until ice crystals form at the edges (or pour into ice cube trays and chill), about 15 to 20 minutes. Chill the bowl and beaters. Whip and use as directed. A 12-ounce package of frozen strawberries may be substituted for fresh.

Contributed by Patsy Lethgo

Lacey's Cookies

1/4 cup of brown sugar
1 tbsp. of coffee/flavoring
3 tbsp. of butter, melted
2 tbsp. of dark Karo
1/2 cup of chopped pecans
1/4 cup of all-purpose flour

Mix the first four ingredients. Stir in the pecans and flour until thoroughly combined. Drop the batter by 1/2 teaspoons 3 inches apart onto a greased, foil lined cookie sheet. Bake at 350 degrees for 7 to 8 minutes or until bubbly and deep golden brown in color. *Cool and remove carefully; they break VERY easily! Look great on a Christmas Cookie Platter!!!*

Contributed by Patsy Lethgo

Walnut Cheddar Apple Bread

1/2 cup of butter, softened   1 cup of packed light brown sugar
1 cup of sour cream   2 eggs
1/4 cup of milk   1 cup of shredded Cheddar cheese
2 cups of flour   1 cup of diced dried apple
1/2 cup of coarsely chopped walnuts 2 tsp. of baking powder
1 tsp. of vanilla   1/4 tsp. of salt
1 tsp. of baking soda

Grease a loaf pan. Beat the butter and sugar in a large bowl with an electric mixer until light and fluffy. Beat the eggs and vanilla in another bowl. Blend in the flour, baking powder, baking soda, and salt.

Blend the mixtures together in the large bowl, alternating between the mix containing the eggs and flour and the sour cream and milk, beginning and ending with the egg/flour mixture. Mix well after each addition.

Stir in the cheese, apple, and walnuts until blended. Spoon into a prepared pan. Bake at 350* for 55 minutes or until wooden toothpick inserted in center comes out clean.

Contributed by Patsy Lethgo

Candy Corn

1 cup of sugar
2/3 cup of white corn syrup
1/3 cup of butter
1 tsp. of vanilla
Food coloring (optional)
2 and 1/2 cups of powdered sugar
1/4 tsp. of salt
1/3 cup of powdered milk

Mix the sugar, corn syrup, and butter in a pan and bring to a boil, stirring constantly. Boil for 5 minutes, stirring occasionally. Remove from heat and add vanilla and several drops of food coloring (optional).

Meanwhile, combine the powdered sugar, salt, and powdered milk. Add all at once to the mixture in the pan. Stir until cool enough to handle. Knead until stiff enough to hold its shape. Shape into triangles, or any shape desired. Makes 1 and 3/4 pounds of candy.

Contributed by Patsy Lethgo

****

Watergate Salad

1 large can of crushed pineapple
1 package of instant pistachio pudding mix
9 oz. of cool whip
Large handful of mini marshmallows
Coconut or nuts (optional)

Mix all ingredients together (may add coconut or nuts). May eat immediately. Kids and guys love this one! May also add ice cream and freeze for frozen dessert. Serve this one partially frozen.

Contributed by Patsy Lethgo

German Amaretto Chocolate Cake

1/2 cup of chopped pecans
1 German chocolate cake mix
1 small box of instant chocolate pudding mix
4 eggs
1/2 cup of water
1/2 cup of oil
1/2 cup of Hiram Walker Amaretto

Grease and flour a bundt cake pan. Sprinkle the pecans on the bottom of the pan. In a mixing bowl blend the cake mix, instant pudding, and the remaining ingredients. Beat well then pour into a pan and bake in the oven pre-heated to 350 degrees for about 40 to 45 minutes.

Cake Topping:

1 stick of butter
1 cup of sugar
1/4 cup of water
1/4 cup of Amaretto

Put the ingredients in a pot and bring to a boil for about 2 minutes. After removing the baked cake from the oven, pour the topping over the still warm cake still in the pan. Allow the cake to cool before removing it from the cake pan. Let the cake set for 24 hours before serving.

Contributed by Homer and Sue Aebi

Laotian Sweet Potato Cake

1 lb. of grapes
1 cup of rum
3 cups of water
1/2 lb. of coconut, grated
3 lb. of sweet potatoes, boiled
1 tsp. of butter
1 tbsp. of oil
Add vanilla, cinnamon and nutmeg to taste
About 1/3 tsp. salt
3 eggs

Soak the grapes in the rum. Pour 3 cups of water into a pot and bring it to a boil, then turn off the heat and add the coconut to the pot and cover. After about 30 minutes remove the boiled coconut from the pot and save it.

Then peel and chop the sweet potatoes and add them to the pot. Boil the sweet potatoes until cooked, then mash completely. Then add the coconut, butter, oil, vanilla, cinnamon, nutmeg, salt, and eggs. Mix them well.

Then add the grapes and rum and mix them in well. Pour the mixture into a buttered or sprayed baking pan and bake in an oven pre-heated to 375 degrees for about 45 minutes to 1 hour.

Rhubarb Cake

1/2 cup of butter
1 and 1/2 cup of brown sugar
1 egg, beaten
1 cup of sour milk
1 tsp. of baking soda
2 cups of flour
2 to 3 cups of rhubarb
1/2 cup of sugar
1 tsp. of cinnamon

Mix all ingredients except the last two and pour into a 9"x13" baking pan. Sprinkle the sugar and cinnamon over the top of the batter. Bake at 350 degrees for 45 minutes to 1 hour.

Contributed by Patsy Lethgo

Philippines Sticky Rice Cake

1 cup of sugar
3 large eggs
1 stick of softened butter
2 cups of milk
2 tsp. of vanilla
1 box of sweet rice flour
2 tbsp. of baking powder
1/2 cup of flaked coconut

Blend together the sugar, eggs, and butter. Then beat in the milk and vanilla. Mix the flour and baking powder together and then add them to the liquid. Stir in the coconut, and then pour the mixture into a buttered or sprayed bundt cake pan. Bake in the oven pre-heated to 350 degrees for about 50 minutes. After removing from oven let set for 10 minutes before turning over onto a plate.

Contributed by Aurora Huston

****

Strawberry Soup Dessert

2 pints of fresh strawberries
2 cups of sugar
2 pints of sour cream
1 pint of half and half milk

Cap all the strawberries and cut them in half. Pour the strawberries, sugar, sour cream, and half and half milk into a blender and blend until the strawberries are in small pieces. Pour into a container, cover and chill in the refrigerator. Serve in small soup bowls for dessert.

Contributed by Pleiku Pals

Strawberry Sauté Dessert Topping

3 tbsp. of butter
1/4 cup of chopped walnuts
3 tbsp. of dark brown sugar
3 tbsp. of grated semi-sweet chocolate
2 cups of halved or quartered premium strawberries

In a medium skillet, melt the butter until bubbly, add the walnuts and stir briefly until the nuts begin to darken. Add the brown sugar and stir for 30 seconds or less. Remove the pan from the heat then add the chocolate and strawberries. Spoon over ice cream or angel food cake.

Contributed by Carl Harris

****

Ice-Box Lemon Pie

1 can of Borden's sweetened condensed milk
2 egg yokes
2 fresh lemons, juiced and partially strained
Rind of 1 lemon, grated
2 egg whites
1 ready-made graham cracker pie crust

Pour the condensed milk into a bowl, then beat in the egg yokes, lemon juice, and lemon rind. Beat the egg whites separately until they are very stiff, then gently fold them into the lemon pie mix. Pour the completed mixture into the pie crust and place under the oven broiler until the top turns light brown to set the mix. Chill the pie in the refrigerator for at least 2 hours before serving. *Note: Must use real lemon juice in this recipe because artificial or reconstituted won't work. The mixture will not set up properly.*

Contributed by H.C. Goodson

Honey Bun Cake

1 box (18.25 oz.) yellow cake mix
4 eggs
1 cup of brown sugar, packed
2 cups of powdered sugar
1 tbsp. of vanilla extract

3/4 cup of vegetable oil
8 oz. of sour cream
1 tbsp. of ground cinnamon
4 tbsp. of milk

Mix the cake mix, oil, eggs, and sour cream in a large bowl. Stir until the lumps are gone. Pour half the mixture into an un-greased 13" x 9" glass, baking dish. Sprinkle the brown sugar and cinnamon on top. Spoon the other half of the batter on top. Swirl a knife through the cake until it looks like a honey bun. Bake at 325 degrees for about 40 minutes. While it is baking, whisk together the powdered sugar, milk, and vanilla. Pour the icing over the warm cake.

Contributed by Cheryl Moody

Oatmeal Cookies

1/4 lb. (1 stick) of butter	1/2 cup of sugar
2 eggs	1 tbsp. of vanilla
1 tsp. of walnut extract	1/2 cup of cocoa
2 cups of flour	1 cup of Quaker Dry Oatmeal
Milk (as needed)	1 cup of semi-sweet chocolate morsels

Preheat the oven to 350 degrees. Combine the butter, sugar, eggs, vanilla and walnut extracts, and cocoa in a large bowl. Add the flour and oatmeal to the mixture until blended well. If there is not enough liquid to mix all the ingredients after five minutes of stirring, slowly add a tiny amount of milk to aid in mixing the remaining ingredients. Taste the batter before cooking, and adjust the amount of sugar to your liking. Add the semi-sweet morsels.

Roll into one inch balls, press on a lightly greased cookie sheet and bake for 8 to 12 minutes, depending on how large you made your cookies. Can be cooked for a shorter time period for chewier cookies, or a longer time for drier, crispier cookies.

Contributed by Melisa Cameron

ABOUT THE AUTHORS

Terry P. Rizzuti was born in Oklahoma in 1946. He spent most of his youth in upstate New York before returning to Oklahoma in 1965. He joined the Marine Corps in 1966, served a tour in the northern I-Corps area of South Vietnam assigned to the 26th Marine Regiment, and was awarded the Purple Heart for shrapnel wounds. Rizzuti graduated with an English Literature degree from the University of Oklahoma in 1977, and then continued on to complete two years of graduate-level literature studies. Currently, Rizzuti is a writer living in Oklahoma. He is working on three novels, as well as trying his hand writing short stories.

R. E. Armstrong was born in a small town in Southeastern Oklahoma in 1948, the youngest son of Scot/Irish and American Indian parents. He grew up in a small town in Southern California a short distance from the border of Mexico. He enlisted in the U.S. Army in June 1967 and served with First Field Force in the Central Highlands of South Vietnam. Armstrong holds a degree in Sociology from the University of Oklahoma (OU), and did graduate-level work at OU in Human Relations. He is a founding member serving on the executive board of OU's Vietnam Memorial Scholarship Association. At this time he is working on a novel and doing research for other future writing projects.

R. E. Armstrong and Terry P. Rizzuti co-authored *Veterans' Benefits: A Guide to State Programs*, Greenwood Press, 2001.

P. O. Box 13218
Maumelle, Arkansas 72113

Index

0-595-34229-9

Printed in the United States
31300LVS00002B/55-57